The
POWER
and the
GLORY

by
Esmond Jefferies

To Doreen

© Esmond Jefferies

World rights reserved by the publishers

Arthur James Limited
One Cranbourne Road
London N10 2BT
Great Britain

First published 1991

British Library Cataloguing-in-Publication Data
Jefferies, Esmond
The power and the glory: the story of a Christian
healing fellowship with case studies
I. Title
265.82

ISBN 0-85305-303-0

Cover design by
The Creative House, Saffron Walden, Essex

Typeset by John Dekker, London N20

Printed by
The Guernsey Press Co Ltd, Guernsey, Channel Islands

The
POWER
and the
GLORY

by
Esmond Jefferies

The story of a
Christian Healing Fellowship
with Case Studies

With a Foreword by
The Rev Dr Richard G Jones

Arthur James

BOOK PUBLISHERS

ACKNOWLEDGEMENTS

In writing this book I have been made constantly aware of the debt owed to all those who have made the experience possible. I think of the many who regularly support our Fellowship meetings, no matter what the weather may be like. Then there are those who give so much of their time in ministering to the sick along with those who work in an administrative capacity.

We are most grateful for the generosity of both the Church Council of Trinity Methodist Church in Felixstowe where we hold our regular meetings and the Church Council of Museum Street Methodist Church in Ipswich which has made available a comfortable room in which we give the ministry of healing to the many hundreds who come seeking Christ's wholeness.

I have, also, to express my gratitude to all those who have given permission for me to write about their individual cases. I have indicated where names of patients have been changed to protect identity, but background details of the cases have been accurately recorded as they have a direct bearing on the problems in need of healing.

The events recorded in the following pages would not have been possible without the constant support of my wife, Doreen, who has been as much involved in the healings as I have. She has ably filled the role of the one who listens to, and comforts, the families and friends who bring the sick to Pin Mill. She, too, has felt the strain that comes with trying to help the seemingly endless flow of people in need of healing. For her constant support, I am eternally grateful. And without the support of all the wonderful friends in the Pin Mill Christian Healing Fellowship, the Fellowship would not be able to function.

Most of all I give thanks to the Divine Healer, Jesus Christ, who has given us all the great privilege of being just a small part of His almighty plan.

Esmond Jefferies

CONTENTS

FOREWORD

By The Rev Richard Jones, MA, BD, DD

There is a crucial place in the life of the Church for systematic theology and exposition. How impoverished we would be without the theologians and their expertise, without that learning which brings to us the wealth of scripture and the outcome of centuries of Christian thought. Without them we could easily become superficial, repeating old slogans, old answers to questions which nobody now raises. How boring!

There is an equally crucial place for straightforward testimony, the freshness of those who tell us of what God has been doing in their lives. By its character, testimony does not attempt to answer every conceivable question that has then been provoked in our minds. It cannot attempt to relate that sparkling series of personal discoveries to every possible aspect of human wisdom. It is not explanation, but experience. It is not some elaborated theory or philosophical treatise or doctrine, but the telling of a story. It may well be for others to work out its full significance for Christian doctrine or Church statements, but without such stories we could easily become abstract, cut off from the immediate work of the Spirit and the marvellous ways in which He is earthed into the everyday. How vital!

So here is testimony for us — rich testimony indeed. The author is widely known as 'Jeff', so here we have the vivid story of what Jeff has found God doing with and through him in the last few years. There is a vitality about it which may well leave us lesser mortals gasping a bit. There is passion, too, a passionate longing that the healing ministry of the Church be released amongst us as it has been in the tiny, charming little hamlet of Pin Mill, down on the River Orwell below Ipswich. Jeff retired there to be able to paint and sail boats, for Pin Mill is a veritable haunt of the artist and sailor. But it was not to be, as the reader will discover.

The testimony is laced with hints about how a healing ministry is practised. What does a person with these gifts actually do? Where does he or she stand, how are hands used, what sort of prayers should be said? It is all here, making this work a little manual of instruction as it goes along. And if we ponder why the stories here tend to emphasise the positive results of such a ministry, with little said about the so-called 'failures' there is a reason, but not much space is devoted to it. The reason is that Jeff simply does not know, nor pretend to know, why in some instances there appears to be quite surprising benefit, and in others nothing at all seems to happen to change a person's condition. There is a mystery at work in these matters, and only the brash rush in with glib reasons ("You didn't have enough faith", "God is punishing you", "God wants most of all to teach you humility and patience", etc).

For, let's face it, the mystery remains. Indeed, in the matter of the healing ministry we are often at the core of much of the fundamental mystery of all human existence. How did God first initiate the whole universe out of the Big Bang many millennia ago? Staggering mystery! How does evil arise in a world made by a loving God? Agonising mystery! How does our redemption in Christ actually work? Glorious mystery! How does Christ rise from the dead? Ecstatic mystery! How does prayer work? Gracious mystery! How do some people, but not all, find healing? Profound mystery! And so it will remain until the end of time. We do not expect Jeff to solve that profound dilemma for us in a few smart pages. We are glad that it is allowed to remain unsolved but set within the certainty of a God who wishes wholeness for us, and time and again giving people marvellous discoveries of it.

Here, then are the marvellous discoveries Jeff has been privileged to share with very many people. But let us note something else. Jeff is not some Spiritual Superman far exalted beyond the rest of God's people. He is a humble, trusting servant, the first to stress that his work is part of the consistent prayer and devotion of a large team of people, The Pin Mill Christian Healing Fellowship, many of whom find similar gifts to Jeff's, and many of whom don't. Yet each of them finds a purposeful fellowship in the total ministry which all, as a big sprawling group, are expressing. For all of this let us thank God!

Richard G Jones

INTRODUCTION

There have been many important periods in my life. The war was, for example, an experience that, to a young man, was an exciting adventure but it is certainly not one that I would wish to repeat.

Meeting Doreen, getting married and bringing up a family provided the solid framework within which the remainder of my life was to take shape. That has had an on-going influence on everything that has happened to me and must surely rate as the most important period. But of the many events that have taken place within that period, the last thirteen years during which I have been involved in the Christian healing ministry have to be regarded as special.

A career in advertising provided an excellent opportunity for me to gain a greater perception of human nature than in almost any other situation. The last fourteen years of that period, when I was running an advertising agency in London, gave me invaluable experience in the art of communication, through endless presentations to clients.

In the pages that follow I have set myself the task of recording some of the events of the past thirteen years. They are events which, I am convinced, have been the work of the Holy Spirit for not one has been planned by those who have been involved. The Pin Mill Christian Healing Fellowship has been formed and Jesus Christ has given us the most positive proof that He lives and heals among us today just as He did 2,000 years ago.

The blind have received their sight, the deaf have been made to hear. Malignant tumours have been healed. Troubled minds have been given the Peace of God. Those who may have doubted have been strengthened in their belief.

Such have been the blessings given to those who have asked for healing in His name, that many doctors, seeing the evidence of these healings, now send their patients to the Fellowship.

Of the great number of books published on the Christian healing ministry, I have yet to find one which gives a detailed, step-by-step account of what the writer actually did when laying on hands. I have, moreover, yet to find a book which gives detailed case studies of the healings of a wide variety of diseases and conditions affecting mind, body and spirit. It is for this reason that I have dealt, in considerable detail, with the way in which I have approached these healings.

I have also described the joy and emotional experiences that have followed some of the healings, for what happens *after* a healing is often as important as the healing itself. It is a part of the total experience. The physical healing has, in many cases, been that which has opened the door to the beginning of a spiritual understanding of the influence God can have in our lives.

It is my hope that, in the pages that follow, I shall be able to give sufficient practical guidance to those who are, at present, actively involved in healing prayer groups and want to take that further step towards the ministry of laying on hands.

The objective of those involved in the ministry of Christian healing must be to bring into creation God's perfect world. This means that we are dealing with the healing of *all* that is sick in our world. As soon as we realise this, it will be seen that there is no shortage of subjects needing attention:

sickness of spirit   *sickness of society*
sickness of mind   *sickness of our planet.*
sickness of body
sickness of relationships

2

The one effective 'treatment' common to all sickness is *prayer*. It is with this in mind that I approach all the problems that are brought for healing — whether it is for physical healing, healing of the memory or relationships or for those who want to be drawn closer to Jesus. Whatever approach I am led to take, it is taken while seeking guidance through prayer. The healings that have resulted will, I trust, have brought *glory* to the Father, whose alone is the *power*.

I wish to make it quite clear that these approaches to healing are those which I, personally, have been led to follow. This does not mean that I believe other approaches to be wrong. God uses His servants in many different ways and it is the way in which He has been using me that I am attempting to share with you in the following pages.

It will be noted that, in some of the case studies, there is a certain amount of repetition. This is to ensure that, if the reader jumps from one section to another, it is less likely that relevant detail will be missed.

To many who have been involved in this ministry for some years, much in this book will appear elementary. To those I say — it is not written with you in mind. I am writing in response to the many clergy and lay friends who, in recent years, have asked the basic but important questions:

> *"How do you start a healing group?"*
> *"What do you actually do when you lay on hands?"*
> *"How do you pray for healing?"*
> *"How do you make the laying on of hands a part of regular Christian worship in the Church?"*

If you, my reader, fall into this category, I pray that you will find something within these pages to take you that step further in your ministry.

Chapter 1

THE GIFT OF HEALING

He arrived at the cottage on time for his appointment — tall, slimly-built and looking rather nervous. His name was Ken and he had been told to come to Pin Mill in Suffolk by the Rev Patrick Ashton, rector of Eyke, who was one of his customers. Ken was his milkman and for the past ten years had suffered from a large malignant tumour in his right forearm. He had been given three courses of chemotherapy and seven of radiotherapy but still the tumour remained. So did the excruciating pain which never left him and prevented him from sleeping. Ken used to swing his arm back and forth as he lay in bed to try to ease the pain, but it never eased. At work he wore a plastic shield to protect the arm and this made work on his milk-round rather difficult. All Ken's customers were concerned for him and when Pat Ashton learned that his arm was to be amputated, he suggested that Christian healing might be of help to him.

So it was that Ken came to Pin Mill on that Thursday morning in December 1982. We talked briefly about his illness and I learned that Ken had little religious experience. I remember him saying, "I've been to three funerals." That was about it! But he had a mind that was wide open to suggestion.

I told him what we were about to do. I said, "In Christian healing we use the power of God which is given to us through Jesus Christ. That power can heal". I explained that all I was doing was acting as a channel for that power and asked him if he would like me to lay my hands on his arm. He said he would like that.

Ken sat in a comfortable armchair with a good head-rest. I placed my hands on his head and said a prayer for the healing of his spirit, mind and body. I then told him to try to banish from his mind any thoughts of bitterness that might be there, thoughts of resentment or anger. If he held a grudge against anyone, he must forgive them. Such thoughts, I explained, are blocks to the work of the power of God and can prevent healing taking place. I then moved my hands down to the tumour on his forearm. After about ten minutes I asked how he felt.

"It's amazing!", he said.

"Amazing?" I asked.

"What I've seen...".

With this brief comment I decided to wait for further details until after the healing. If it seemed interesting, I could then record Ken's experience on tape. This I did and this is what he told me.

Ken felt 'a very warm heat' going into his arm. He then saw two rather indistinct figures coming towards him. This was followed by a bright light appearing in the sky. Beside his chair stood a man.

As he sat in the armchair with his eyes shut, Ken said, "The man had a bright light upon his head and before him he held a big stick, a stick as tall as he was. The man just stood there, looking down with a smile".

Ken added, "His white robe was so bright. It was as though he was watching over us. He was so bright and large, so lit up from the sky. He gradually faded away."

At that moment the pain left Ken for the first time in ten long years. He was still sitting in the armchair when I asked him what he made of the vision. He thought for a moment, buried his face in his hands and said, "I think I've seen Jesus Christ."

I said, "I think you have."

Ken then added, "Something has been taken away from

me and I feel all clean and beautiful inside."

Within three weeks the tumour in his right arm had gone. His only worry was how to explain this to the consultant at the local hospital. He need not have worried. When he examined Ken's arm the consultant asked him to give some reason for the absence of the tumour. He was overjoyed at what he saw and this resulted in the beginning of an unusually close working relationship between the consultant, the sister, the ward staff and the Pin Mill Christian Healing Fellowship.

When I tell of healings such as this, I am invariably asked how I became involved in the ministry of healing. How did it all start? Perhaps it would be as well if I answered that question before going further into the experiences with which so many wonderful friends have become involved.

One Sunday morning in July, 1976, the minister of our church in Bromley, Kent, was speaking of the tragic illness of a brother minister with whom he had trained. John had cancer and his wife had been told that he had two months to live. He was only 45 years of age and they had three teenage boys. The distress of the family was understandable and they were looking for help.

I remembered a colleague at my office telling me how his wife had been to a 'healer' for her troubled back. Doctors had told her that she would be spending the remainder of her life in a wheelchair. But she was healed. We therefore gave details of the healer to John's wife, Joan, and an appointment was made for him to visit the lady. This presented a slight problem as John was in hospital in London and the healer, Mary, lived in Surrey.

My role seemed quite obvious. I ran an advertising agency in Kensington. I had my car in town, so I would take the afternoon off, collect John from the hospital, pick up our respective wives on the way and end up at Mary's house.

When I arrived at the hospital and met John for the first time, I was struck by the frail, grey figure sitting on the end of his bed and waiting for me to take him away. It was my first encounter with cancer.

The staff nurse impressed upon me that John must take one of the tablets every four hours, otherwise the pain levels would rise and would become difficult to control. He had just had seven litres of fluid drained from his pleura where the tumour was.

The journey went well and we arrived at Mary's on time. I had intended just to sit in the car and wait, but we were greeted so warmly and all invited to join her for the healing. Mary would not mind if I describe her as a rather amply built lady with blond/white hair. Her clothes, too, were ample for she liked to be warm during the laying on of hands.

We were led into her sanctuary which she had named after St Theresa. It was quite a small room. There was one large armchair which faced a small, simple altar over which hung a painting of Jesus that had been given to her by a grateful 'patient'. Wherever there was a horizontal surface, one would find a statuette of a saint or the Virgin Mary. I learned later that these had also been given to her by those who had received healing through Mary's hands, many of them nuns.

John sat in the armchair, my wife, Doreen, and Joan sat on canvas chairs and I sat on the only remaining seat — a small wooden stool. Mary placed her hands on John's head and said a prayer for his healing. After about three minutes she opened her eyes, looked directly at me and asked, "Have you been to a healing before?"

I told her that I had not and she continued with the healing for about thirty minutes. During a brief conversation afterwards, she turned to me and said, "You can probably

7

heal. I felt a lot of power coming through you."

This was the last thing I would have expected anyone to say to me — of all people! I muttered something like, "We'll have to talk about it sometime."

Mary suggested that John was brought back to her during the following week for further healing. So once again the four of us set out to visit her, little expecting what was to follow. As before, John sat in the armchair with Mary sitting behind on a high stool. After about five minutes Mary looked at me and told me to try to make my mind go blank and to turn and face the wall.

"If anything happens to you, tell me," she said, and promptly started to tell the story of a completely paralysed woman who was healed during her recent healing tour in Australia. With all this going on it was very difficult to make my mind go blank, but, after two or three minutes, she was quiet again and I decided to turn back on my stool and join the others as nothing seemed to have happened to me.

Doreen nudged me and asked in a whisper, "Anything happen?"

I had not seen any flashes in the sky or heard strains of the Halleluiah Chorus, so I said, "No, nothing."

It was at this point that I was aware of something like an electric current passing through my hands and fingers. I told Mary what I was experiencing and without a pause she said, "I thought so. Come over here. You put your hands on his chest and I'll place mine on his back".

There was no arguing with Mary — so that is what I did. She told me that I was 'channelling' the power of God, which is given to us through Jesus Christ, the Healer.

It is on an occasion such as this in one's life that one's faith has to be examined. Did I believe Mary's explanation of what was happening?

Early Days

I was brought up in a Christian home. Until his later years I can never remember a time when my father was not a member of the choir in the local Anglican Church. In my teens the church was the centre of our social life as well as worship. It was a new church, St Mary of Nazareth in West Wickham, Kent, and it was an exciting time. We built the church hall first, and all the events, both worship and social, took place in this part of the complex. When the funds were available, the church was built onto the existing buildings. My particular role was to form the Scout troop, the 44th Beckenham. Then came the war. I joined the Royal Air Force and flew Spitfires in a fighter reconnaissance squadron. It took me through Belgium, Holland and into Germany. In Germany we were based at Celle, just south of Belsen concentration camp. The horrors of that place I shall never forget.

During my service in the RAF, I was confirmed by the Bishop of Exeter, but when I left the service in 1946, I found myself a very unsettled young man. Although no longer in the Air Force, I spent a great deal of time in the mess at Biggin Hill, just a few miles from my home. It was during this period that I was invited to spend a weekend with an old RAF friend at his home in Broadstairs. That weekend his young sister, a nurse at Great Ormond Street Hospital for Sick Children, came home to celebrate her twenty-first birthday — and that was that! We became engaged and her father, the Rev W R Chapman, MC, a Methodist minister, married us in November, 1947. I was adopted by the Methodist Church — and my father-in-law lived with us in Pin Mill until his death in January, 1991, at the advanced age of 97 years.

Although my roots were well and truly in the Christian faith, they had a decided upheaval during the war, but came back 'on track' when it was all over. When Mary told me that I was acting as a channel for the healing power of the Holy Spirit which is given to us through Jesus Christ, I did not find it a wholly unbelievable phenomenon. I did, however, find it difficult to understand why this was happening to *me*. Since it was happening however, I felt privileged and happy that it was to be of benefit to those in need of healing. Little did I know the demanding time that lay ahead.

Healing of Cataracts

After the second visit to Mary, I arrived home anxious to use this new-found gift of healing. My father-in-law had lost all sight in his left eye, so this, surely, must be a good place to start. We discussed the matter — that I was merely a channel for God's healing power, which, as Jesus had promised, would be given to those who, having faith in Him, lay their hands upon sick people in His name and the sick would be healed. It all seemed so very simple. My father-in-law sat in a comfortable armchair. I sat behind him and laid my hands on his head and asked him to relax. I did my best to relax too. I prayed aloud, confirming my belief that Jesus is with us when we meet in His name and asked that the power of the Holy Spirit pass through my hands and heal the blind eye. At this point in my ministry I was not aware of the great importance of the healing of the spirit and the mind. In fact I was aware of so very little.

After about ten minutes he said that he could see some light — some slight vision which appeared to be developing in the outer corner of his blind eye. We finished the healing by saying, "In the name of our Lord Jesus Christ, be healed."

Believing that some improvement was bound to have taken place — after all, Jesus said it would — I held up a newspaper with large headlines and with difficulty he was able to describe some of the letters and shapes which were held in front of him. "But," he said, "why is everything in

10

my other eye so bright? The whites are so much brighter and the colours so clear."

I told him that I had no idea and asked if he knew why this should be. He told me that he had a peripheral cataract on that eye and now it appeared to have gone.

I did not even know that he had had a cataract on that eye and it had been healed in about ten minutes by the laying on of hands. To me this was a sure sign that Jesus knew what our problems were, even if we did not. It was also evidence that I was no more than the lowliest of instruments in His hands. I did not even know what was being healed as it was actually taking place.

What happened next in my thoughts cannot be explained by anything approaching logic. It was this... If a small cataract can be healed as simply as this, how much more readily a really well developed cataract would yield to this power. But how does one set about finding a subject with a well developed cataract? To walk up to someone in the street and ask if they know of anyone with a well developed cataract was tempting, but hardly acceptable!

Here was I, running an advertising agency in London and, at the same time, finding that, by placing my hands upon sick people, they became well. And it was all happening within a very short time.

What followed next was the occasion when I first became aware of the amazing organisation, planning and power that Jesus can have in our lives if we allow Him so to do.

A week or two later, Doreen and I were driving back to our home in Bickley after visiting friends in Sevenoaks. One of the other guests at the party had missed her last train home. She lived near us so, as we had come by car, we invited her to join us on the journey home. This she happily accepted. During the journey the conversation turned to healing and I mentioned my search for someone with a really well developed cataract. The lady in the back of the car said, "You can have my husband. He's got cataracts on both eyes.

11

He is almost blind and waiting for surgery at Lewisham Hospital."

I almost exploded with delight. The problem was solved and I had found my subject — not just one eye but two — and almost blind!

"Wonderful!" I exclaimed, with such enthusiasm that my wife rebuked me for showing delight at the plight of the poor man.

Let me just pause at this point, because, in retrospect, I now know how important this experience was. My problem had been to find someone with a well-developed cataract. Doubts about the subsequent healing of the cataract had never entered my mind. All I had to do now was to arrange for the man to come to my home for the laying on of hands.

"Will you ask your husband if he would like his cataracts healed — and if so, will he come to me so that I may lay hands on him?" I asked.

The following day a telephone call told us that her husband, Charles, would be happy to come to Bickley and have his cataracts healed, but it would be necessary for me to collect them as they had no transport.

I called at their house on a cold, wet winter's night in November. They were both ready and waiting for me. Charles, who was about seventy years of age, tall and slim, took my arm and I led him out to the car as one would lead a blind person.

When we arrived at our home, Charles sat in an armchair in front of an open fire. I explained to him that the power of God could heal him and restore his sight and that I was simply a channel for that power by the laying on of hands. I sat behind him and placed my hands on his head. After a spoken prayer for his healing, I placed my hands over his eyes. The fingers of my right hand were over his right eye and the fingers of my left hand over his left eye. After about ten minutes I drew my chair round to his left side so that I could place my left hand over his face, covering both eyes, while my right hand was placed at the back of his head. I do not know why I did this — it just seemed the right thing to do. As I did so I was immediately aware of the perspiration running down the back of his head. My hand was dripping wet. I asked him if he was feeling alright, and he told me that he was so hot that we would have to stop and give him an opportunity to recover.

I was disturbed that the laying on of hands had caused such discomfort, for I was yet to learn that, on some occasions, the whole body of the person receiving the ministry can be so drenched in perspiration that a complete change of clothing becomes necessary. So I told Charles that I would sit behind him, place my hands lightly on his head and restore him to a state of comfort and that the heat would leave him. After a few moments his wife became excited.

"He's healed. I know he's healed. I can see he's healed" she cried.

She became even more excited so there was only one thing to do. I picked up a paperback and gave it to him to read. Charles took the book over to the light and proceeded to read it without difficulty.

During the years since that healing I have learned that those who have been blessed with physical healings in this way are very often quite calm about it. I believe that, in many cases, a spiritual revelation takes place at the time of the physical healing. This outward expression of calm gives no hint of what must be taking place in their minds.

Charles read from the paperback and returned to his chair. I laid my hands on his head and we said a prayer of thanks for his healing.

I remember well the journey when I drove them both back to their home. Charles sat in the front passenger seat and spent the journey reading the number plates of cars in front of us as the headlights of my car picked them out. I missed the turning into the road where they lived and it was Charles who spotted my mistake. The healing of the cataracts was

13

confirmed by the hospital and Charles had regained his sight without the aid of a scalpel.

If only my approach to healing today was always as sure and simple as it was on that occasion...

I was at the beginning of what was to become a most busy and varied ministry. I had laid hands on John, the minister, as Mary had instructed me, and he needed no more pain-killing tablets. The fluid began to disappear from his pleura. Next, I had laid hands on my father-in-law's eyes and the cataract had vanished. There was no doubt in my mind, therefore, that the next time I laid on hands, the condition would be healed — and it was.

I had yet to learn that healing does not always happen as we ask, and I had not experienced the inevitable mind-searching when healing does not take place.

Although it is only natural that we should question and research the results of a healing that does not happen as we had hoped and expected, during the act of laying on hands is not the time for such thoughts to occupy our minds. When our hands are laid upon a sick person, our minds must be still, at peace, unquestioning, surrendering completely to Jesus Christ. He may then use us as channels in the way that will give greatest benefit to the sick.

When the healing power is felt to be flowing through our hands it is, however, helpful to ask the sick person what they are feeling. Such questions, when directly related to the healing taking place, create no block. They are helpful in telling us where to place our hands and it also adds to the expectancy in the mind of the sick one.

But after laying on hands it is important to give thanks for whatever may have resulted — for God will have heard our prayers and will be answering them in His own way and for our own good. It is both constructive and healthy to seek and pray for understanding so that we may become better channels within Christ's healing ministry.

During the next two years a number of people came to me for the laying on of hands. They began to telephone me at my office. I well remember the occasion when my secretary, who knew nothing of my involvement in the healing ministry, looking very puzzled, said, "There's someone on the phone asking to speak to the healer!" It made things a little easier when she knew and could take these calls for me. People came during lunch time and after the close of business...and many of them were healed. But an advertising agency is not the best place in which to lay on hands.

Chapter 2

RETIREMENT AND MINISTRY

Doreen and I had been talking about the way in which we would approach retirement. I was 59. We had a boat and we both enjoyed sailing, so it seemed a good idea to start exploring those parts of the country near the sea. We would then avoid those long, seemingly endless journeys to and from the boat during weekends.

We spent two weeks looking around East Anglia for the retirement home of our dreams. Either the house we found was acceptable but the setting was not, or the setting was fine but the house was not. Then, one day, the colleague who had introduced us to Mary when John was in trouble, came into my office with an advertisement from the property column of *Yachting World*.

"Here's your cottage, Jeff," he said, and gave me the advertisement which contained a photograph of a most delightful house. The details explained that it was a Victorian terrace of four dwellings that had been converted into one. It was set in an acre of garden with a stream running through it. And, of all places, it was at Pin Mill on the bank of the River Orwell. It was too good to be true. We went to see it and it was all the advertisement had claimed it to be... and, in fact, far more.

Albert Cottage gave us everything that we were looking for in retirement and the only house in the area which could accommodate all that was to develop in our ministry during the next eleven years. How many gardens of a small cottage could take over twenty cars? And how many converted to provide one large living room big enough — well, almost big enough — to take more than sixty people? But I am leaping ahead.

We moved into Albert Cottage on a cold, wet day in November, 1979. I, stupidly, had agreed to continue at the agency in London for a further year, so most of my time seemed to be spent travelling between Ipswich and London's Liverpool Street Station, with the added frustration of the Circle Line on the Underground to get me to High Street, Kensington. I do not think I saw one smiling face on those journeys, particularly on the tube trains. Everyone seemed to be suffering under a great weight of depression. When I think about it now, I probably looked like that myself!

The cottage had been used only at weekends and holidays by the previous owner. This meant that much of our spare time had to be spent in repair and decoration. One thing I had always wanted was a room in which I could indulge in my painting without having to put everything away between sessions. Doreen had a bright idea. "Why don't you convert the lean-to on the other side of the garage into a studio?"

That is exactly what I did. Although I do sometimes find time to paint, the studio has been, and still is, used mainly for the ministry of healing. It is a place which has witnessed some quite remarkable healings.

During the following six months, one or two people, knowing of our involvement in healing, began to find their way to Pin Mill.

In April 1981, I shook the dust of London from my feet and began to relax.

The Church shows Interest

I recall an occasion during coffee after a Sunday morning service when Doreen and I had been to the local Methodist chapel. The minister, the Rev Michael Corney, had given a thought-provoking address and had talked of the healing ministry of Jesus. I spoke to him about this and asked when he was going to include the ministry of healing within the worship of the church. Michael was aware of some of the healings that had taken place at our cottage and he began to

17

ask searching questions — the sort of questions that can lead to the fulfilment of Christ's total command to us to "to go forth, preach the Gospel *and* heal the sick." But this was not the occasion on which to get into deeper conversation on such a far-reaching and important subject. Coffee mornings after church do not provide the necessary time for discussion of that nature.

It was some months later when Michael came to me and said, "Do you remember talking to me about the ministry of healing?" I said that I did. "Well, at our last Circuit staff meeting the subject of healing came up." he said. "None of us seemed to know much about it. I told them that you were already involved in this ministry, and the Superintendent has asked if you will come to our next meeting and give a short talk on the healing ministry." Knowing that there are many other 'ministries' of healing which are not Christ-centred and anxious to avoid becoming involved in such activities, Michael added, "At least we know where you've been!!"

I accepted the invitation to speak at their staff meeting. This was the first time I had been asked to speak on the subject of healing and it was to a group of about nine Methodist ministers and their Superintendent.

I was certainly no biblical scholar, so I had no intention of becoming involved in any deep theological discussion. What I could do, on the other hand, was simply tell of my own experiences in healing in the name of Jesus — and leave them to form their own conclusions. The truth of what I was to talk about was evident in the healed people who could, if necessary, be called upon to testify.

The very thought of my talking to a group of clergymen caused Doreen to have grave doubts about my sanity! She was, understandably, afraid that I would get out of my depth, but such thoughts did not worry me because I was going to keep rigidly to the events within my own personal experience.

Driving to the meeting, along the road beside the River

18

Orwell, I was able to gather my thoughts. I was very much aware that this was the first time I was to confront the 'professionals' on their own subject. I needed guidance, and, being alone in the car, I had an opportunity to talk with the Divine Healer and seek His help. "Be with me at the meeting, Lord," I said aloud. "It's your meeting, Lord. Be in my mind, in my tongue and in all I do."

As I drove under the Orwell Bridge, I had a further thought. I added, "If you think it's a good idea, Lord, and there is someone present who has a bad back or stiff neck and comes forward for the laying on of hands, all those present will see how the power of the Spirit heals."

I arrived at the manse little realising that this was to be one of the most important meetings of my ministry — if not *the* most important.

They were all there when I arrived. My talk was to occupy the second half of the meeting. I started by telling them how I became involved in the healing ministry. I told them how one event had led to another and I gave details of some of the healings. I also explained what I did in the laying on of hands.

Having over-run my allotted time by ten minutes, there was no opportunity for questions. But, as I was about to leave the meeting, one of the ministers, the Rev Reg Edmonds, stood up to ask a question. "Ah!" I thought. "Here is the bad back that I asked for — or perhaps it's a stiff neck."

It was neither. "I have a friend who needs help," said Reg. "He is the music master at the big comprehensive school in Ipswich and he has had a serious accident which has resulted in severe loss of sight. He can't see to read or write. He has been suspended from duty at the school and his wife has to drive him about and escort him wherever he may have to be."

I had prayed for someone to come forward so that those present would have evidence of the power of the healing

Christ. But just see how that prayer had been answered! Not a mere bad back or stiff neck but a man nearly blind! Being a teacher at a school with 1,400 children, all of whom would have known about the accident, meant that there was now an opportunity for all those children and their parents, to witness his healing. If that was not divine intervention, I do not know what is!

The Blind given Sight

I asked Reg Edmonds to make sure that his friend made contact with me and asked all those present to join me in committing ourselves, in prayer, for the healing of this man and the restoration of his sight. I then left the meeting.

The man, Russell, came to see me one Sunday morning at the beginning of May. His wife brought him and left him with me for about an hour. He told me that he had been using a photocopier at the school and it had malfunctioned. The cover had been raised and it had flashed its 600 watt, tungsten halogen lamp right into Russell's face and eyes. Within a short time his vision became badly affected.

Recalling the moment of the accident, Russell said, "It was as though I had been looking directly at the sun and the main, central part of my vision had been destroyed."

He went on to explain that one eye was much worse than the other. He then told me that he had been to the Institute of Neurology at The National Hospital in Queen's Square in London, where he had a brain scan. The verdict, after much examination, was that the optic nerves and the receptor cells at the back of the brain had been damaged. Russell was told that nothing could be done to repair a damaged optic nerve or the brain cells and that he should prepare himself for future years of blindness.

Having told me the story of how it happened and the medical prognosis that he had been given, I laid hands on him asking for the healing of his spirit, mind and body. I suggested that he came to see me on the following Friday.

Russell's next appointment was in the afternoon. I was seeing someone in the studio earlier that afternoon and as she was leaving, I walked into the garden with her. There, standing by a poplar tree, waiting for me to collect him, was Russell. His wife had brought him and left him there while she went off to do some shopping.

I took him into the studio and sat him down in the big armchair facing the windows, which, to the sighted, gave a splendid view of the garden with its weeping willows, poplars and fruit trees. I remember the occasion well because the poplars were bending in the breeze and the leaves were flickering in the bright sunlight. It crossed my mind that Russell could see none of this. The room is 24 feet by 13 feet. It has a wooden floor and windows as large as I could make them to give me the maximum light for painting. In the centre of the roof are three large, clear corrugated plastic panels to provide even more light.

This was fine for painting but the studio was to become a healing sanctuary. Or, as one wit called it, a sort of 'ealing studios'!

Russell sat in the big chair and I sat behind him. He had told me that his sight was no better since that first visit but he did feel much more at peace.

I placed my hands on his head and said, "I give this healing in the name of our Lord, Jesus Christ." Next, I said a prayer for the healing of Russell's spirit, mind and body. During this prayer I could feel the power coming through my hands. I next placed my hands over his eyes for about four or five minutes. This was followed by placing the fingers of my left hand over his left eye and my right hand on the back of his head, a little to the right. I understood that this is where the receptor areas of the brain are located. My hands were therefore at both ends of the damaged optic nerve. After a further five minutes I repeated this on the right eye. It was during this time that I asked Russell how he was feeling (remembering Charles who became so uncomfortably hot during the healing of his cataracts).

Russell said that he felt something happening between my hands. He appeared to be disturbed by what he felt because he brought his own hands to his head and placed them over mine. I took my hands away from his head and moved round in front of him. He looked up at me and said, quite calmly, "I can see you. I can see everything. I can see the grain of the timber beams — the weave of the curtains..."

I took an art book from the shelf. It was *A Canvas to cover*, by Edward Seago. I turned to one of the chapter headings where there was some rather small print. Russell covered one eye with his hand and read the small print without difficulty — and he was not wearing the glasses which he had worn for the past twelve years.

I said, "Now try reading it with your bad eye."

"I've got news for you," he replied. "That was my bad eye!"

I went into the cottage to find a piece of music for him to read. If he could do that, he was back in his job teaching music at the school. Somewhere in the house we had the score of Handel's Messiah. If I could have turned to the Halleluiah Chorus, I felt it would have been most appropriate! But it was not to be. All I could find was a book of nursery rhymes set to music which had been given to me by an aunt on my fifth birthday. I gave the book of nursery rhymes to Russell and he read the music without difficulty. Jesus had given us that for which we had asked. We gave thanks.

We waited for Russell's wife, who was due to come and collect him, but she was late, so we wandered down the track beside the cottages to meet her. As we waited by the river, I noticed Russell looking at the clouds scudding by. He was looking at all that was going around him. An aircraft flew over and he looked at it as though he had never seen one before. Still his wife had not returned, so rather than just standing there waiting for her, Russell decided to walk up the lane to meet her. I left him and returned to the cottage. I have often wondered what was in his wife's mind when she saw Russell walking towards her... unaided.

The story of Russell's eye condition and the subsequent healing, is told by Dr Rex Gardner in his book, *Healing Miracles — a doctor investigates* (Darton, Longman and Todd). Dr Gardner obtained access to Russell's medical notes from Ipswich Hospital. For those wishing to know something of the medical details, this account could be of interest. Dr Gardner concludes his investigation by quoting from a report by the neurologist which was sent to Russell's GP, and then comments on the report:

> The neurologist wrote to the GP: "This man's vision, as you know, has returned completely to normal following a visit to a *faith healer. He even says he has no need for glasses. I can find no defect. Presumably the relaxation from his visit to the faith healer has abolished persisting cerebral vasospasm in the occipital cortex.

Dr Gardner then comments:

> Although this may be the complete answer, we have seen that the explanation for the blindness was conjectural and unique. What is clear is that some fifty days after the loss of vision it returned suddenly and completely during believing prayer. However, what confirms to me the miraculous nature of the cure is that the patient's vision did not return to its pre-accident state — he had needed glasses for twelve years — but was restored better than before, so that he no longer needed them."

As I have already mentioned, 1,400 children and their parents knew about the damage to Russell's sight — and now they knew about his healing.

That event began a whole series of developments — talks to prayer groups and church councils of various denominations, etc. All of this developed into the Fellowship we have today.

Those ministers who were present at the Superintendent's

staff meeting, at which Russell's damaged sight was first mentioned, now had first-hand proof of the power of the living Christ in the ministry of healing.

My prayer, as I drove under Orwell Bridge, had been answered.

*Note: When people call me a 'faith healer' I correct them. I am **not** a 'faith healer'. I am a channel for the healing power of God given to us through His Son, Jesus Christ. If I have to be called anything at all, it is more correct to use the term 'Christian healer'. Faith healing can encompass those who have faith in themselves or another human being, their doctor or the pills he has prescribed. Christian healing, which seeks the wholeness of spirit, mind and body, can only be achieved through trust, faith and belief in Jesus Christ.*

Chapter 3

A FELLOWSHIP IS BORN

A few weeks after Russell's healing I was asked to speak at a meeting of a prayer group organised by Reg Edmonds, the minister who had put Russell in touch with me. It seemed appropriate that I should invite Russell to join me at the meeting. He could tell his own story and answer the questions which were bound to arise. It has been my experience that, where possible, having at such meetings, people who have been healed through the laying on of hands does help others in their belief and understanding of the healing ministry.

This meeting was the first of many such meetings — and it has been from occasions such as these that The Pin Mill Christian Healing Fellowship has grown. During discussions on healing and how Jesus heals today, just as He did 2,000 years ago, often someone present begins to feel 'something strange' happening to their hands. So it was that, a few days after that first meeting, I received a letter from Pam Hulford, a local preacher in the Methodist Church. In her letter she wrote:

> ...During the meeting at Reg Edmond's home, when you were speaking, I experienced this tingling in my hands. In sharing this experience at our Class Meeting, a member asked for the laying on of hands for a back problem and the Lord was able to channel His healing power through me. Subsequently, we have seen wonderful things happening, both as a result of prayer and laying on of hands...

Through this and similar experiences we now have a team

of twelve people who regularly lay on hands during our meetings and at healing services in churches. As more people received Christ's healing touch, so interest in the ministry began to grow. I think it was Reg who asked, "When can we meet and discuss what is happening?" The date was fixed for September 17, 1982 — the first meeting of our Fellowship. Before we left that meeting Reg took out his diary and asked, "When are we going to meet again?" and added, "I'm not leaving until we've fixed a date!" So good was it to see such enthusiasm that we started coming together for meetings regularly every two weeks.

During the following month I was invited to speak to a group at Trinity Methodist Church in Felixstowe. The minister, the Rev Patrick McCluskey, was one of those who had been present at the Superintendent's meeting when Russell's blindness was mentioned. About fifteen people came to Trinity that evening and we met in one of the vestries. Sufficient interest was shown for a number of those present to ask if they could come to our next Fellowship meeting at the cottage in Pin Mill. About seven people attended that meeting and as people came forward to receive healing, I invited Patrick to lay on hands. This was something that he had never done before, but he has since become a most effective channel for the healing power of God.

The Crowds gather

The meetings in Albert Cottage became more widely known as we were blessed with more healings. More and more people came until our living room was bursting at the seams. On more than one occasion we had over seventy people. Those who came early occupied the chairs. Others were lucky enough to find cushions on which to sit while the rest simply sat on the floor. Those who could not get into the room sat on the stairs.

These were truly memorable occasions and such happy ones. Just looking at the solid mass of people gathered together in the name of Jesus Christ, one could well imagine what it must have been like two thousand years ago when the crowds gathered around Jesus. We were doing the same today. The differences in religious persuasion were forgotten and at one of our meetings we had Anglican, Methodist, United Reformed, Baptist and Roman Catholic priests and ministers all worshipping and praying for the healing of the sick under the same roof. One Church! One God!

On more than one occasion, when we had as many as twenty people come forward to receive the laying on of hands, some were healed without human hands touching them and without even leaving their seats. Gwyneth arrived for a meeting and said she wanted to receive healing for a very painful back condition. When the time came for her to come forward she announced that she no longer had a problem. As she sat there praying for the healing of those who went before her, she felt the pain being relieved. I like to imagine that Jesus, whom we know to be with us when we meet in this way, looks around the room and, seeing the crowds gathered, decides to give some direct assistance by walking among His people and laying His blessed hands upon them.

I remember the evening when Kwini came to the meeting. Kwini came from Malawi. She had married an Englishman who was farming in her native land. Sadly, her husband had developed a malignant tumour in his brain, so together with their young family, they came to live in England where the necessary medical treatment could be given. Kwini came forward to receive the laying on of hands by proxy for her husband.

We had three armchairs in which people could sit to receive the laying on of hands, with two of our healing team at each chair to give the ministry. Kwini sat in one of the chairs and prayers were said in a low, quiet voice for the healing of her husband as hands were laid on her head. Others had occupied the two remaining chairs and hands were being laid on them also. As usual, although there were about sixty people in that room, there was not a sound to be heard. A wonderful peace settled upon all those present. Suddenly, Kwini let out a piercing cry. It was as though she was calling to God for help in her anxiety over the illness of her husband. Her cry froze us all and it was a moment or two before we realised what had happened. Kwini continued her sobbing cry to God.

Sitting on the floor, a few yards from Kwini, was a man who had not been to our meetings before. He was dressed casually, like most of those present. While the rest of us remained still and silent, the man on the floor rose to his feet, stepped over others who were also sitting on the floor as he made his way to Kwini's side. He bent down a little so that he could speak quietly into her ear. As he did so Kwini stopped sobbing and a wonderful peace came upon her.

It was not until after the meeting that we learned what had taken place. Our 'stranger' was a Salvationist missionary on leave from — of all places — Malawi. When he spoke to Kwini in her distress, he said the Lord's Prayer in her own dialect. We had never seen him before, and we have not seen him since that day. I am in no doubt that our Lord knew of the very special need we would have for the man from Malawi.

Growing Pains

Because of the growing number of people attending the meetings, some of the regular supporters of the Fellowship suggested that they should no longer come. They felt that they were taking the space that could better be occupied by the sick. For these faithful supporters not to attend was unthinkable. We needed their prayers and support as much as we needed those who laid on hands.

A solution to the problem was provided by the Rural Dean of Woodbridge, Canon Frank Hollingsworth. He had a small, eleventh century church which was only used very occasionally. He told us that we could have it for our meetings if it was suitable. Would we like to come and see it? We wasted no time. Frank and his wife, Pam, Doreen and I, together with Sally (a lady about whom I shall be writing later), jumped into our cars and made for Culpho.

St Botolph's Church, which can seat about fifty people, is located in a country lane in Culpho, near Woodbridge. It is a delightful church, surrounded by a few houses whose occupants look after the church's needs. The main one is to prevent it falling into a state of decay! It had no water supply, so all refreshments would have to be brought to our meetings. Electric power was available, however, so we would have heating. There were no toilets — and this would present problems, particularly for those who came from places as far away as Cambridge or Colchester — and many did. There was no car park. In spite of these difficulties, we decided to make St Botolph's one of the healing centres of our Fellowship.

People came to our meetings from far and wide. How they heard about us I shall never know, for we avoided any form of publicity like the plague!

St Botolph's has a tower with a single bell, and my immediate thought was to ring the bell with every healing and let the good news of the living, healing Christ ring out over the countryside. We did ring it, just that first night, and immediately realised it could cause a problem for those who retire to their beds at an early hour! So the bell remained silent at future meetings. A pity!

To begin with we decided to alternate our meetings between Albert Cottage and St Botolph's. The third meeting in the church was attended by well over sixty people. There were not enough chairs so they were sitting on the font steps and even on the stone floor. Then we had a visit from the police. They were most polite about the whole matter, but made it quite clear that so many cars parked in the lane were causing an obstruction and they could not allow this to continue.

At the next meeting I counted eighty people in St Botolph's. That forced us to make a decision. We could no longer continue to meet in this lovely old church and so we came back to Albert Cottage and to the same old problem of space.

Our meetings at the cottage continued for a further four months, after which we held our first meeting in the church hall at Trinity Methodist Church in Felixstowe.

We join CCHH

Shortly after this I received a telephone call from The Rev Denis Duncan who was, at that time, the Director of the Churches' Council for Health and Healing. He had heard of our work and asked some questions about our Fellowship. He then suggested that we might consider becoming members of the Council. Being an ecumenical fellowship we felt it necessary to talk with Anglican and Methodist church leaders in East Anglia before taking this important step. With the blessings of The Rt Rev John Waine, Bishop of St Edmundsbury and Ipswich, and The Rev Richard G Jones, Chairman of the Methodist Church's East Anglia District, who were both most helpful and encouraging, we became members of CCHH.

Now that we were becoming more actively involved on a wider base, we invited a dear friend, the retired Bishop of Portsmouth, The Rt Rev John Phillips, to become our President. In spite of a long period of ill-health, John accepted this appointment and was there to guide us on the path we were to follow, until his death a year later. Still in need of that guidance at the head of our Fellowship, we invited Richard Jones to give us that lead. Today he is our

President and, in spite of the many demands on him, he somehow finds time to come down from Norwich to attend our meetings.

Chapter 4

THE WAY WE LAY ON HANDS

It may be helpful at this point, to explain how we conduct our healing meetings.

First, and most important, there has to be a planned structure to the meeting, otherwise it can get out of hand and go on far too long. It has to be remembered that many people attending may be in severe pain and can only remain seated for a short time — and much depends upon the quality of the seating.

At our main Fellowship meetings we place a large carpet in the centre of the floor. This helps to soften the environment and make it less like a traditional church hall. We are fortunate in having some excellent curtaining which not only helps the appearance of the setting but it also helps the acoustics. About seventy chairs are placed around the edge of the carpet. Some are comfortable armchairs to accommodate those in need of extra support. At each of two facing ends of the carpet we place armchairs and a third is placed on one of the remaining sides. Each of these is attended by two of our healing team. It is important to ensure that these armchairs have open sides, so that if it becomes necessary to place hands on the lower back of the sick person sitting in the chair, access to their back can be gained through the open sides.

In the centre of the carpet is a small table on which is placed a cross. Beside the cross is an open book in which are written the names of the sick who are unable to be with us and for whom prayers of intercession will be said during the meeting. Beyond the circle of chairs is a display of books on various aspects of healing, which may be borrowed.

Just before we start the meeting, those who are to be involved in the laying on of hands retire to the vestry. There we are led in prayer, asking that Jesus Christ fills us with His power and that we may be channels for His healing love. We then ask that those who come to Him for healing may receive relief from their suffering.

In our experience, ninety minutes is the maximum time people can endure being seated in this way — and this has to be broken up with different points of interest. We start the meetings at 7.30 pm with a few words of welcome. We then explain, very briefly, for the sake of those who have joined us for the first time, the form the meeting will take. This is to ensure that no one will be sitting there wondering what is likely to happen next.

One of the Fellowship team gives a short address in which is explained our approach in the search for wholeness through Christian healing. It is made quite clear that Jesus Christ is at the centre of all we do.

We are reminded how Jesus spoke with His disciples, when He said:

> I tell you the truth, anyone who has faith in me will do what I have been doing. He will do even greater things than these because I am going to the Father. And I will do whatever you ask in my name so that the Son may bring glory to the Father. You may ask me for anything in my name and I will do it.   (*John 14:12–14*)

We emphasise that those who come for the laying on of hands should do so putting their faith wholly in Jesus, believing what He said and expecting to be healed.

It helps at this point to ask for a show of hands to gain some idea of the number of people coming forward. In this way we are able to decide how long we can give each person. It is usually about ten minutes. It also enables us to decide whether to have the refreshment break after the prayers of intercession or to continue with the laying on of hands and have the refreshments at the end of the meeting. (It is useful to have a clock in view as many of us find that, when giving this ministry, we tend to lose all sense of time.) This done, those in need of healing are then invited to occupy the three chairs to receive the laying on of hands.

At 8.30 pm we link in prayer for the healing of those whose names have been written in the book beside the cross. Each name is mentioned with a brief description of the sickness to be healed and, in anticipation of that person's healing, we visualise them being given the healing for which we have asked, restored to full health in spirit, mind and body. Then, as already explained, if there are only two or three more to come forward, we continue with the ministry, or, if there are many more, we break for refreshments allowing people to stretch their legs.

At the end of the meeting another of the team leads us in a prayer of thanks for the blessings received during the evening.

Healing in Pairs

Another regular meeting place we are fortunate to have is Museum Street Methodist Church in the centre of Ipswich. Counselling is an important part of healing but cannot be achieved in the short time available at the main Fellowship meetings. At this church we are able to give each person as much of one hour as may be needed. In addition to this, the number of people seeking healing is such that, having this venue, the whole 'healing team' of twelve can be employed on a rota basis, when a man and a woman are on duty in the morning and another couple take over in the afternoon.

On these occasions it is important to ensure that at least one of the couple on duty has plenty of experience in dealing with the wide variety of disorders that present themselves. At this church we meet in a pleasant, warm room which contains a comfortable armchair and a specially constructed couch which we find is ideal for relaxing people, particularly when laying hands on backs and hips.

Healing One-to-One

There are those who come with intimate problems which can best be dealt with on a one-to-one basis. Speaking to more than one person gives them the feeling of being out-numbered and the intimate, personal contact, so important in building trust and understanding, can so easily be lost. The studio in the garden at Pin Mill is ideal for such counselling.

At one end of the studio is a simple wooden cross which is mounted on a white background. In a corner is a large wood burner — essential on cold winter days. It also creates a cosy, friendly atmosphere, which is a great help when people arrive for their first visit, apprehensive and nervous. In addition to the large, comfortable armchair I have a couch on which people can lie when the need arises. As a matter of fact I find that people can relax more easily when they are on the couch than when in the chair — and relaxation is so very important if healing is to take place. The couch is also used when teaching people how to relax. But more about that later.

There are two comfortable chairs for those who may have accompanied the one in need of healing, but more often than not people seem to prefer not to have others present during the laying on of hands. I, too, prefer this as the sick person can then concentrate wholly on what is happening and not be distracted by the thought of an 'on-looker'. It is only natural that, if I am laying hands on a woman and it is her first experience of this ministry — and the first time we have met — she is quite likely to be a little apprehensive. I know this is so because people have told me. And if that lady's husband is sitting with us, her mind will probably wander towards her husband and what his thoughts may be in, what is to them, a most unusual situation. On the other hand, if the couple are committed Christians who are in the habit of praying together, they will ask to be together during the healing. This I welcome.

Frequently the sick person will be with me in the studio while others of his or her family are being comforted by Doreen in the cottage. It is quite surprising how a cup of tea, a sympathetic ear and perhaps a shoulder to cry on, can relieve tension and, at the same time, provide valuable information about a situation which has a direct bearing on the healing of the sick partner.

Chaperoning

We now come to the delicate subject of the chaperoning of ladies who arrive for the laying on of hands. When they come to a church service or where more than one person is giving the ministry, there is no problem. But when a lady is to receive healing and counselling on a one-to-one basis and the one giving the ministry is a man, it is a different matter. The danger for the counsellor is that some ladies with emotional problems may 'fantasise' and the counsellor become an innocent victim of her imagination with far-reaching and damaging results. Recognising that there are many occasions when people wish to be seen alone, I endeavour to safeguard myself in two ways. Firstly, I pray about it and ask for protection against such an unfortunate event. Secondly, when anyone phones for a first appointment, I always ask how they have heard about the work of the Fellowship and how they obtained my phone number, in order to give me a little background about them.

If the lady is married, it is both helpful and reassuring to ask for her husband to be present at the first meeting. Christian healing should then be explained together with the manner in which we lay on hands. They should be asked if they are happy with what they have been told before the ministry is given. I have yet to come across anyone who does anything but welcome this approach. Finally, I ask the lady if she would like her husband or anyone else to be present during the healing but I have had very few cases in which the wife wanted her husband to be present or, for that matter, the husband wanted to be with us.

While on the subject of dealing with potentially 'delicate' cases, it is as well to mention those who come with psychological problems that require deeper counselling on a one-to-one basis. It is both wise and helpful to ask if they mind the session being recorded on tape. It can be explained that it is then possible to concentrate wholly upon their problem without the distraction of having to take notes. People understand this and so we have a full record of the session that can be studied at a later date. It also acts as a safeguard against the possibility of becoming a victim of fantasy. However, *never record a session without that person's knowledge and approval.*

Having explained the importance of chaperoning when women come for the laying on of hands by a man, I must emphasise that the same caution should apply when a man is receiving the laying on of hands from a woman.

Healing within a Church Service

Before explaining how we conduct our healing services in church, I must commend to the reader a book by John Richards, *The Question of Healing Services*, a Daybreak book published by Darton, Longman and Todd. This book deals in detail with many aspects of healing and different approaches to it within a church service.

In our own experience we have found it is better to combine the laying on of hands with Holy Communion, firstly, because healing can take place through the sacraments, and secondly, because some people find it embarrassing to stand and come forward for the laying on of hands in front of a church full of people. They have an uneasy feeling that others in the congregation may be wondering what could be the matter with them. But they have no such feelings about coming forward to accept the bread and wine. When the laying on of hands follows the giving of the sacraments, people seem less self-conscious about coming forward for this ministry.

The conventional procedure is for the minister, having given the bread and wine to those who are kneeling at the altar rail, to pass along the row again, laying hands on those who may request it. The difficulty with this is that the minister may not be aware of the problem to be healed. His prayer in such cases is, therefore, likely to be of less help to the sick person than it would be if he had an opportunity for a brief word before giving the ministry. Another disadvantage of giving the ministry in this way is that it is almost impossible to lay hands on the ailing part of the body, a practice which we find gives great benefit to the sick person.

It is for these reasons that we place two (sometimes three) chairs at one side of the altar rail, where those in need of healing can sit comfortably, explain their problem without their neighbour hearing every word, and receive appropriate healing prayer with the laying on of hands. This allows the communion service to continue without interruption.

Some who attend healing services may well be of different denominations and for others, entering a church may be a rare occasion. To avoid embarrassment, the ideal situation is to provide a printed form of service, a duplicated sheet which can indicate when the congregation is expected to sit, stand or kneel, when hymns will be sung, when the address will be given and when the laying on of hands will take place, etc.

Another important item of management is to ensure that there are plenty of stewards, appropriately name-tabbed, to greet people as they enter the church and to answer questions of those who have come for ministry. It may well be that some, arriving by themselves, sick and in pain would welcome a steward or other member of the church to sit with them. It must be remembered that Christian healing begins with caring and this is where the whole church can play such a vital role.

During the service we arrange for the hymns and Bible readings to be related to Christ's healing ministry and the address provides an opportunity to prepare those who are deciding whether to come forward for the laying on of hands. Towards the end of the address, the minister explains that people may come forward to receive the bread and wine and the laying on of hands. If they wish to receive one without the other, they may do so.

Finally, we ask those who wish to receive the laying on of hands to come forward in the first wave of people, (whether they are receiving the sacraments or not), and occupy the first pew. This assists us in two ways. It enables us to have some idea of the number of people who are to be given the ministry and also provides a place for them to wait for it to be given.

Before the congregation receives the sacraments, those who are to give the laying on of hands come forward as a team and receive the bread and wine together with the minister. He then dismisses them, "In the name of Jesus Christ, go forth in the power of the Spirit and heal the sick"

The laying on of hands may continue during the final hymn after Communion.

A small point which seems to worry some who lay on hands in churches concerns the state of their hands. I have in mind those occasions during the winter when the church may be cold to start with, within a few moments, when the ministry are as cold as the pillars and stone walls that surround them. There is a fear that this will prevent them from being the effective channels which they hope to be. I have even seen people searching for warm radiators to cling to before the service. In my experience, even though hands may be cold to start with, within a few moments, when the healing power is given to the sick person, the hands will become warm. I can recall occasions when, although my hands have been cold, the person upon whom I had laid them told me of the extreme heat being experienced. To worry about the state of one's own hands is therefore quite unnecessary. Such concern can only act as a block to the flow of the Divine healing power.

The congregation is invited to join us for refreshments in the church hall after the service and this provides an opportunity for people to discuss their problems more fully with those who have ministered to them. It also allows those who have more intimate problems to step aside from the crowd, open their hearts and, when necessary, make further appointments to receive the ministry of healing.

The Harvest is plenteous, but...

It is my belief that there are prayer groups all over the country very eager to take that extra step forward and lay on hands. But what should they do? How should they start? With these and many more questions to be answered some of them join us at our meetings on the first Friday in the month at Trinity Methodist Church. They witness our simple approach. They see the relaxed manner in which we conduct the meeting and they see people being healed. It is usual for us next to receive an invitation to attend one of their meetings, to give them that little extra support and confidence needed to take the all-important step forward.

Such was the case with the Methodist Church at Heartsease Lane in Norwich. They record their experience as follows:

> We would like to share with you how God has been leading our Church to form a Christian Healing Group. It all started in the autumn of 1987, when the leader

40

of the Wednesday Bible Study Group, Stanley Rise-borough, felt led to obtain the Pin Mill tape on Christian Healing, which the Group studied during that time and into Spring 1988.

We felt so inspired by the tape that we arranged a visit to a Pin Mill Fellowship meeting at Felixstowe. Eighteen members of our church went along and found it a profoundly moving experience. We were all very impressed by the love and care shown by those laying on hands and the great feeling of peace and simplicity throughout the evening.

We then submitted a report to our Church Council and they agreed to our inviting the Rev Patrick McCluskey to talk on healing in our church in September, and to have Jeff Jefferies come to our church in October to help train the members of our Healing Group in this work.

There was a tremendous response to this October meeting — our Epworth Room was overflowing with 66 people present. About half were from seven other churches in the District, even though we had not advertised the meeting.

Jeff Jefferies and Helen Cavanagh both took part in laying on hands and told us of many wonderful healings since their work began in Suffolk.

Since this meeting we have had remarkable accounts of healing from people who were present. A lady with breast cancer found on her return home that the lumps had gone; a man with asthma found it much improved; a little girl with eczema was completely healed; our minister, the Rev Peter Edwards, found his bad neck much better. We again reported to the Church Council who agreed that we should go ahead with the Ministry of Christian Healing.

We met on November 25 when members shared their experiences of healing and, led by Peter Edwards, we planned the way forward. It was decided that we should hold an Open Healing Meeting on Saturday, December 17 in our main church hall, and although we are all still very new at laying on hands, we feel it is right and that God is leading us to do this. We plan to hold a meeting in January to monitor our progress and in February to hold an Evening Communion Service with the laying on of hands.

Please pray for us in this very exciting venture which the Lord has already blessed in abundance and we feel sure will do so in the days ahead.

Rosalind Sorrell

Chapter 5

KEEPING IT SIMPLE

It has been my privilege to have taken part in healing services in many churches. Although the manner in which the ministry has been given has differed, the objective has always been the same. It has been a prayer that those seeking healing should be led towards a state of wholeness of spirit, mind and body.

Whichever approach is adopted, it is very important that those who are involved in the ministry are completely at ease and comfortable in what they are doing. It is equally important that they have absolute belief in what they are doing. It is no good just hoping for the best. If we truly believe that which Jesus told us, then we can do nothing but believe. How many times I have heard people say, "I do believe that healing can take place, but I find it difficult to believe that it can happen to me." Comments of this kind have been voiced by those seeking healing as well as those who hope to channel Christ's healing power.

This is an area from which many clergy appear to hold back. They seem to do so for one of a number of reasons. Some find it very difficult to identify with this part of Christ's ministry, and although Jesus instructed His followers to "Preach the gospel and heal the sick", they decide to have no involvement in the second part of His commission.

Others have said that they would be afraid that nothing would happen, in which event they would appear rather foolish in the eyes of their congregation and lose authority within their church. This is a very honest and understandable reaction. Unfortunately it is born of a lack of understanding of the role of the one who lays on hands. As soon as it can be realised that Jesus is the healer, that no healing power originates within us and that we are merely channels through which Jesus works, then the responsibility for the healing of the sick ceases to be ours and is handed over to our Lord.

The commission to preach the gospel and heal the sick was given by Jesus to his disciples and so becomes an essential part at the centre of the Christian faith. It follows, therefore, that every church should be a healing fellowship. Every member of a church is capable of being involved — in prayer, in caring, loving towards each other, listening to those with problems, counselling, the laying on of hands. I am sure there are many other ways in which Christ's love can be shown to those in need.

Having said this there arises the question of who should lay on hands in the church. Without hesitation I say that every ordained person should lay on hands, whether or not they believe they have the gift of healing. They do so in obedience to the command Jesus gave to His disciples (Matthew 10:5 – 8). They should do so on behalf of every member of the healing church.

Within the church there will be those, other than the minister, who have a 'gift of healing'. This is something over which the recipients of this gift have no control. It is frequently recognised by a strong tingling sensation in the hands, and often brings great surprise to those concerned! It is a gift given to the church as a whole, and those used as a channel for this power have a responsibility to ensure that it is centred within the authority of the church.

Now a word on preparing oneself before laying of hands needs to be given.

The question is often asked: "Is it necessary to fast before ministry?" My own feeling about this is that is *not* necessary. I base this judgement on the possibility of being called to lay on hands in an emergency. In such a case I would not have been fasting and I know that God would not deprive anyone in need of healing just because I had not fasted. On the other hand, it makes good sense not to have a large meal within two or three hours before laying on hands. If I have a full stomach, I find that I am not physically comfortable and my body is, of necessity, concentrating on the digestion of that food. It has been my custom for some years now to have only a light snack, making sure that it is something that can be digested easily.

Another question concerns private prayer. Before starting a day of giving the ministry to people, it is essential to have a few minutes, at least, alone during which we offer ourselves as channels for God's power and that our minds may be emptied of our own thoughts and filled with God-given wisdom to discern.

In some groups, hands are laid on a person without those involved in the ministry being aware of the sickness to be healed. In others, hands are laid on the head and shoulders of the subject and no other part of the body. While some feel that these approaches to the ministry are right for them, I have to confess that I feel more in tune with the subject when I have had a brief talk with them before laying on hands. I first ask their Christian name, by which I refer to them in prayer. I then ask a simple question, "What is the problem?" Knowing the answer to this question I am better able to understand the needs of that person and can express this in the prayer for their healing. I ask them to relax as much as possible and to allow their arms to flop by their side with their hands placed limply, palms upwards, on their lap. I quite often suggest that they become limp like a 'rag doll', so that they may surrender themselves in body, mind and spirit to Jesus.

I next lay hands on the head of the sick person, making sure that my arms are also relaxed. Sometimes I can rest them on the back of the armchair when it is high enough. I keep my fingers together and make a positive contact on their head with the fingers and palms of my hands. It is important not to put downward pressure on the head as this will cause discomfort and even pain.

Healing Prayer

When the healing is given within a church service, I speak quietly, close to the person's ear. Whenever possible, and particularly when giving the ministry to someone who is receiving it for the first time, I give a full prayer for their healing. As I have been asked many times about healing prayer, let me now give you the prayer that I find is of help in most situations. I will call the person to receive the laying on of hands, John, and imagine that he has a severe pain in his lower back. I want you to notice that within the prayer, I explain to John why I am praying in this way.

I give this healing to you, John, in the name of our Lord, Jesus Christ. I say this so that no power other than that of God, which is given to us through His Son, Jesus, can be used in your healing.

Let us remind ourselves of a promise that Jesus made. He said... "When two or three are gathered in my name, I will be in their midst". (Matthew 18:20) ... You and I are met here in His name, so we can be quite sure that He, in a way that we do not understand, is here with us. I want you to shut your eyes and just imagine the three of us — you, me and Jesus, the Healer, standing by the chair — the same Jesus who healed people when He walked among us 2,000 years ago, and has been healing us ever since. This being so we can talk with Him.

Lord, we come to you asking for the healing of John; the healing of his spirit, his mind and his body. Lord, we first ask that his spirit be made strong, that it be renewed and that his faith and dependence upon you grows stronger day by day. We ask, Lord, that you give your peace to his mind. Help him to banish from his mind any thoughts of bitterness that may be there — bitterness about events of the past. (Pause.) Help him to banish from his mind any thoughts of resentment, jealousy, anger or hatred. (Pause.) Thoughts such as these, John, are blocks to the work of the Holy Spirit within us and can prevent healing taking place.

And there is something else which is equally important: if there is anyone against whom you hold a grudge, anyone who has done something hurtful to you and needs your forgiveness, no matter how long ago it was, now is the time for you, deep down in your heart to say, quietly within yourself... "Lord, I forgive them." ...and mean it.

Let us now ask for the forgiveness of your sins. Lord, we ask that you forgive John all his sins, that he be cleansed and renewed in spirit and mind and fit to receive the healing power of the Holy Spirit. We ask for that power to descend upon him, to fill him and to make him whole in spirit, mind and body. We think particularly of John's back and ask that the cause of the pain be washed from his body and that he be fit and free from pain and able to live an active life in your service.

Now, John, we remind ourselves of another promise that Jesus made — in fact the greatest promise made in the history of mankind. When Jesus was preparing his disciples for the time when He would no longer be with them, He said: "I tell you the truth. Anyone who has faith in me will do what I have been doing. He will do even greater things than these, because I am going to the Father. And I will do whatever you ask in my name so that the Son may bring glory to the Father. You may ask me for anything in my name and I will do it." We have asked for your healing, John, in the name of Jesus who told us the truth. Let us profess our faith in Him and now accept your healing so that God may be glorified according to the word of His Son, Jesus Christ.

During this prayer, in which I am asking for the power of the Spirit to be given to John, I, as do most others involved in the healing ministry, begin to experience a tingling feeling in my hands. This, I have come to recognise as a sign that God's healing power is being channelled through my hands in answer to my prayer for the healing of John.

I ask John to let me know if he feels any sensation in his body while my hands are on him, no matter how slight, from the top of his head to the tip of his toes. I want to know what is happening within him and I am waiting for him to tell me that he feels a heat and a tingling in a particular part of his body, or, it may be, all over his body. I am careful not to suggest what sensation he may feel, otherwise he may imagine it or say something just to please me.

When John and I both feel the power coming through, I know that he is receiving the healing power of God in accordance with the promise Jesus made. This gives me a wonderful feeling of confidence and a positive attitude of mind in which to lay on hands — and this cannot be bad!

I say that "this cannot be bad" because I am convinced that the state of mind of the person giving the ministry can be transmitted to the person receiving it. This is why it is so important that we, who lay on hands, should find it within us truly to believe what Jesus said: that anyone who has faith in Him will do the things that He has done... and really expect the sick person to get well, just as he would have done if Jesus was laying His hands on him. After all, it is still Jesus who is directing the power, so why should we not expect the sick to get well?

On the other hand if we lay on hands, saying one thing and believing another, we not only create a confused channel through which the power of the Spirit may work but we also transmit this confusion and negative attitude to the mind of the sick person.

One other point that needs to be made is that, during the

healing prayer and after, there is no need to close our eyes. If our eyes are closed we cannot see what is happening around us, least of all what is happening to the one seeking healing. By watching the face of the sick one we can learn a great deal, particularly if we are dealing with someone in pain. As the power is being given to John, I talk with him and rejoice in what is taking place.

Dealing with the Problem

At this point, feeling the power being channelled through my hands, I move to the side of the chair and place one hand on John's back where he feels the pain — having first asked him to remove any heavy or bulky clothing. If the painful area is beneath a belt, I ask him to loosen the belt so that I may place my hand on his back without the distracting feel of the belt beneath my hand. I then place my other hand on his abdomen so that my hands are either side of the trouble spot, front and back, when I visualise the power of the Spirit passing between my hands, healing as it does so. Had it been a painful knee, I would have placed one hand on the knee and the other at the back of the knee. After about two minutes, I ask him to tell me if he feels anything where my hands are, and if he feels any sensation, no matter how slight, in any other part of his body, to let me know.

The sick person can very often be most helpful by commenting on the progress of the healing. In Mark 8:22–25, Jesus has to ask the blind man whether he can see anything, and from his reply, Jesus realises that more healing is required and again places His hands on the man's eyes. The man then tells Jesus that he can see.

In the case of our patient, John, he will almost certainly tell me that he feels a considerable heat at his back. He may go on to say that it feels as though the heat is penetrating his body and going between my two hands. Whatever he tells me, I say, "Good. Tell me if any other feelings develop."

I may give him some idea of what to expect, by telling him that the heat could increase; it could become less; he could even feel a sudden cold spot. I also tell him that the pain could become more intense; it could become less or it could even move about his body. In my experience it could do any or all of these things.

Let us assume that this is a difficult and obstinate back condition. In some cases the pain will increase and become almost unbearable. This is no time to stop as it would leave John in great pain. It is at times like this that one's faith is tested. On such occasions I remind myself, and John, that we are using the power of God. He is giving to him that for which we asked, and what John is experiencing is the 'battle' that is taking place between the power of God and the condition which is causing his back pain. I tell him that he can be quite sure who is going to win that battle and to let me know when the pain reaches its peak and begins to lessen. It is not long before John's body relaxes and he tells me that the pain is beginning to go. We give thanks to our Lord. I tell John to let me know when he feels no pain. It is important that I keep my hands on John until all the pain has gone. He tells me that all the pain has gone but he is afraid to move. I tell him to have no fear, the battle has been won. Jesus has given him that for which we asked. I ask John if he would like to say a prayer of thanks. If he finds that difficult, I say the prayer for him.

Giving Healing to a Child... Eczema

Giving the ministry of healing to a child should be kept as simple as possible. Try to imagine the way in which Jesus would handle the situation.

The first thing we have to do is to gain the friendship and confidence of the child. Let me explain by the following example.

James, a little boy of six and a half years, was brought to me suffering from eczema. His eyelids were so encrusted that it was difficult for him to open and close them. His whole body was covered with these painful sores which always seemed to be more painful at bed-time. They would itch and he would scratch. They would then bleed and become more painful and he would cry out in pain. This went on night after night.

James sat in the big chair in the garden room. The tiny figure was almost lost in that chair, and when I asked him how long he had had these nasty sores, he looked up at me and said, "Since I was born." It was as though he was saying, "Since the beginning of time."

In talking to him about the things he would like to do, but could not, his love of football came out on top. I talked to him briefly about Jesus and His great love of little children and said, "Would you like me to ask Him if He will take away all your sores so that you can run about and play football like other boys?"

My question met with a very positive, "Yes, please."

When a child is capable of understanding what is happening there is little point in praying aloud in terms with which the child cannot identify. Far better to create for him a mental picture of the way in which he is being healed.

I told him to shut his eyes very tight and keep them shut. I then asked him if he would like me to ask Jesus to take away all the nasty itching. By putting this question — which may *seem* unnecessary — it is involving the child in making the decision to go to Jesus for healing and it helps the expectancy of the healing to come.

I then suggested to James that we asked Jesus to take out of him all the nasty itchings and take them away so that they would not hurt him any more. I explained that I would place my hands on the tops of his arms and very gently squeeze out, through his fingers, all the itchings. As I did this we would ask Jesus to take all the itchings away. Again, before doing another thing, I asked if he would like me to do this. He began to build a mental picture of what might happen and asked "Will it hurt?"

I assured him that nothing would hurt. "Oh, good," he said.

I ran my hands gently down his arms, over his head and face, down the front of his body and his legs. James reminded me that I had not put my hands on his back, so he leaned forward so that I could run my hands down his back also. When I had completed this laying on of hands I started to pray, asking aloud that Jesus would take away all the itchings from James's body. The little boy began repeating my words (I had not asked him to do this). So I continued, asking Jesus for the healing of his spirit and that he should grow up to be a big strong boy. I then told James to open his eyes and asked, "How was that?"

He replied, "I can't feel anything."

All the pain had gone, so I suggested that he said 'thank you' to Jesus, which he did — in the simplest of words: "Thank you, Jesus."

James went to bed that night without pain, and his parents slept well without the sound of his usual cries. He came to see me on two more occasions when his mother told me that he came to her one morning and said, "Look, Mummy, no blood on my pillow."

Learning of his passion for football, I had placed a football on one of the beams in the garden studio and told him that he could have it as soon as he was completely clear of sores and was able to run about. This gave him the added mental drive, in the most positive terms, to look for his healing. Each morning he would look at himself in a mirror and ask his mother, "Has it gone enough for the football?"

Within a few weeks James was clear of the sores he had had since he was born, and the day came when he was given his football. He lost no time kicking it about in our garden with his young brother.

(James's grandmother lives with James and the family. One day, some considerable time after his healing, he saw his grandmother scratching her knee. James stopped her, saying, "Don't scratch, Granny. Pray!")

The Power of the Spirit

When the healing prayer has been given and the power can be felt coming through one's hands, the power of the Spirit is sometimes shown by its effect upon the sick person.

I have already mentioned Charles who had a healing of his cataracts and who became so hot that I had to give him time to recover. At a meeting of a healing group in a local rectory, I was asked to lay hands on a man with back trouble. He was a tall, well-built fellow who had received his back injury when playing rugby. He did not really want to come forward, but his wife, who had already received healing, gave him a push and he found himself sitting in the chair, very sceptical about the whole procedure. I placed my hands on his head and prayer for the healing of his back. Next, I placed one hand at his lower back and the other at the front. He immediately said that he could feel a heat passing between my hands. Within about two minutes I felt water dripping on my hand which was placed over his stomach. Perspiration was running off his face. The man was saturated. A few days later I had a phone call from him asking if he could come and see me. His back pains had been healed and he no longer had any doubts about the power of God.

On another occasion I was sharing a healing service with The Rt Rev Richard Hare, Bishop of Pontefract. He had given an inspiring address on the healing Christ and offered to anoint those who wished to come forward. Within a few moments a queue formed down the length of the aisle. After being anointed, those who wished to receive the laying on of hands sat in a large wooden chair. I remember one man —

he was about sixty — told me that for years he had felt divorced from Jesus, and wanted me to pray that he could be drawn closer to Him. This I did and, as the Spirit filled the man, he shook so violently that the chair began to move.

This phenomenon, although perfectly natural within healing, can sometimes be a little disturbing within a small meeting in a confined space. I have found that, if it continues longer than would have been expected, it can be calmed by saying aloud: "The peace of God be in you. The peace of God calm you. The love of Jesus fill you and give you His peace." Repeating this, or a similar prayer, brings peace to the person seeking healing and the shaking lessens until it stops. (I advise you to have a glass of water at hand as it will most likely be needed.)

More frequently, however, the healing power of the Spirit causes a mild heat and a tingling sensation to pass through the body of the sick person in the region of the troubled area.

There are also occasions when the power of the Spirit, passing through the healer causes the hands to shake. This is an uncontrollable shaking which varies in its degree of violence and can be disturbing when laid on the head of a sick person. I recall the occasion when Gwyneth, who was new to our healing team, and a powerful channel, was sharing a healing session with me at the church in Ipswich. Her hands were shaking too much to be able to place them on the head of the sick person. Before seeing the next person we talked about it, believing that in time, her body would become accustomed to channelling this power and that it would stop.

The ever present Christ was aware of the problem and when the next person came forward Gwyneth's hands were as steady as a rock.

The Healing Light

During some healings, although the person's eyes may have been shut, they will say they saw a light as they received their healing, a light far brighter than the sun, but it did not hurt their eyes. I explain that this was the 'healing light' that is seen by some people when healing is taking place. When the cancer in Ken's arm was being healed, he saw the light and described it as a blazing bonfire.

Sally came from her doctor suffering from a twisted spine and in great pain. It had been like this since the birth of her last child. After the laying on of hands and she was without pain for the first time in four years, she asked, "What was the brilliant light that I saw when your hands were on my back?"

We talk of the Light of Christ and in The First Letter of John 1:5–7 he tells us that "God is Light": and in 1 Peter 2:9, he tells us that we are God's people and that we are to praise Him and give witness to his bringing us 'out of darkness into His marvellous light'. So what was seen was evidence of the presence of God in Christ who healed them.

The Light lifts Depression

Raymond came to me having suffered from deep depression for 22 years. In the morning he would awaken with a dark shadow surrounding him and his whole body was consumed in fits of violent trembling and drenched in torrents of perspiration. He was on heavy medication which did not seem to resolve the problem.

When he had finished telling me how wretched he felt, I told him that the power of God could take away his depression. He looked at me with despair written all over his face and said, "Mr Jefferies, I don't think I believe in God any more."

"Don't worry," I said. "He still believes in you. After all

55

He created you so He must believe in that which He created."

Raymond looked at me and burst into tears. I simply sat behind him, placed my hands on his head and asked Jesus to take Raymond in His arms and lift him out of the darkness and into the light — God's Light.

He came to see me again the following week. For a moment I did not recognise him. He was smiling, indeed almost laughing, and when I asked him how he was, he said, "I'm frightened that it may not be true."

He went on to tell me how he had been going about work in the garden singing and that he had even enjoyed helping his wife with her shopping.

If, as sometimes happens, the sick person does not receive the relief expected during the laying on of hands, it should be explained that healing continues for some time after the ministry has been given. I have heard it said by those who have received healing for a bad back pain, for example, that it felt as though they had had a hot water bottle at their back for three days, after which all the pain left them. In other cases, the day after receiving healing can prove to be painful, but after three days all pain goes.

To help in the building of belief and expectancy of healing, I offer the following prayer:

Lord Jesus Christ, I know that it is your wish that I should be whole in spirit, mind and body. I also know that the healing power of God, our Father, can and will make me whole.

Lord, help me to accept my healing by showing me how I can be drawn closer to you, so that I may live my life according to the way you have shown.

Chapter 6

FAITH, BELIEF AND EXPECTANCY

I cannot emphasise too strongly that the details of my approach to healing through the laying on of hands must not, in any circumstances, be regarded as a 'formula' for the healing of the sick. This, or any other prayer or approach to healing, is likely to be effective only if it is given in faith in Jesus Christ. In addition to this it is essential that the one laying on hands really does believe that the healing will take place, keeping in mind the promise that Jesus made, that anyone who has faith in Him will do the things He had done and that, whatever we ask in His name, He will give to us. If this belief is not present in the mind of the one laying on hands, the channel through which the power of the Spirit may be given to the sick person, may well be blocked.

We come now to the faith of the one seeking healing. If he or she has belief in the absolute power of God and that his or her healing will take place, so much the better. Unfortunately this is not always the case. If the recipient finds it difficult to have that belief even though they know that healing can and does happen to other people, they will probably find themselves having faith in the person whose hands they can actually feel touching their body. This is easier to believe.

So long as recipients are made to understand that the power given comes through the grace of our Lord, and if the mind of the person giving the ministry is centred wholly on Jesus, then I do not believe that it matters too much if their faith is, to begin with, a little misplaced. But when the healing has taken place, it is quite remarkable how understanding begins to develop. This is, I believe, how someone is led towards wholeness — first the healing of the body, which is given as a sign of God's love and power through Jesus Christ, then the healing of the mind, when realisation of what has happened begins to occur, and finally, the renewal of the spirit, resulting in the wholeness which should be the objective of all Christian healing.

The following case is a perfect example of how faith, belief and expectancy can lead to healing.

And the Deaf shall hear

Sharon was twenty years of age and secretary to a consultant at Ipswich Hospital. Let her tell her own story:

Fifteen years ago at the age of five, I contracted mumps. I got over the illness but was left completely deaf in my right ear. This is a rare side effect and is even rarer that the deafness should be permanent. I visited the London hospital every two years to make sure that the trouble did not affect the other ear. They told my parents that, as the problem was in the inner ear, it was incurable.

Recently I became aware of an 'emptiness' in my right ear and decided to seek alternative treatment. A colleague at the hospital told me of the healing ministry at Pin Mill, so I made an appointment.

I went confident that I would come away with two good ears. After all, I had told my boss and others in the department that I would be returning with two good ears.

After Jeff had explained to me what he was about to do, I lay on the couch and he sat behind with his hands on my head. All at once I felt a surge of power sweep through my body. Jeff prayed for the healing of my spirit and then of my mind. He then moved his hands to my ears and began to pray for the healing of my body, asking God to put back the good hearing that I was fortunately given at birth. I was asked if I could feel any sensation anywhere in my body. I replied that I could feel tingling and warmth in my right ear; it was explained that this was caused by the healing power of God. I then felt that the deafness was being drawn from me and the hearing being put in its place.

I don't know how long Jeff's hands were on my ears, perhaps ten minutes or so. He took his fingers from my right ear and then blocked my left ear with his other hand. I could hear everything. Previous to this I could hear nothing in my right ear. It was such an emotional experience. I cried with relief and joy. My parents were waiting for me outside and Jeff called them in. Both parents were relieved and overjoyed that all was well. Before this, my parents were worried that I might be expecting too much, so didn't talk about it but now it is the only thing they do talk about! They were so pleased and relieved that I had been healed.

I believe that going to Pin Mill with an open and confident mind and not being afraid, made it easier to accept what was happening to me. I think that if you believe it will happen, then it will. Healing might not happen straightaway, but in time good health will return. This really does prove there is a God and that if He is asked in the correct way, He will help those who need Him.

Sharon wrote that testimony as soon as she returned home from Pin Mill. I can only guess what her feelings must have been like. But my own feelings — I know what they were like! This is an example of how faith and expectancy prepares the way for the work of the Holy Spirit. Sharon had told the consultant for whom she works and others in the department, that after receiving the laying on of hands she would return with two good ears. That is an expression of faith rarely seen.

Sharon and I talked for over half an hour about the way in

which Jesus had healed people 2,000 years ago and how He was still healing them today.

When she lay on the couch, I placed my hands on her head and prayed for the healing of her spirit, mind and body. I told her that Jesus was with us and to imagine Him standing by the couch. I placed my right fingers on her right ear and my left hand cupped over her left ear so that she could hear what I was saying (we had to remove those big gold ear rings!).

At the end of that prayer and when the healing power could be felt by both Sharon and myself, I was reminded of the way in which Jesus has healed the man who had been deaf from birth. I explained, with my fingers still on her ears, that the man had been brought to Jesus when He was surrounded by a large crowd of people in Galilee, and Jesus was asked to heal him. But Jesus knew that when his hearing was given to him for the first time in his life, if the noise of that crowd was to be his first experience of sound, it could be most distressing for him. Jesus therefore took him aside from the crowd, where it was quiet, and prayed to His Father asking to be given the power to open the man's ears. When He felt the power in His hands, He knew that the man would be given his hearing, so He placed His fingers in the man's ears and gave the command for them to be healed. The word He used, I explained to Sharon, was an Aramaic word, *Ephphatha* which means "Open up". The man's ears were opened and he could hear.

At this point I removed my hands from Sharon's ears and she spoke those three beautiful words, "I can hear!" I placed my finger, hard on her left, good ear and asked, "Can you hear me now?"

"I can hear everything." she said. As she sat up the tears of joy flowed. The box of tissues came out. She trembled with emotion. I hugged her tight and we said, "Thank you, Lord. Thank you for giving to Sharon that for which we asked."

For the first time since she was five, she could hear where sounds were coming from. More tears and laughter — her mother and father had not yet returned from their drive around the nearby lanes. I wanted Doreen to share in the joy of this healing, so I hurried into the cottage and said, "We've just been given a wonderful healing. Come into the studio and meet Sharon."

When we arrived back in the studio, Sharon was still sitting on the edge of the couch, still the tears streamed down her face as she laughed with sheer joy. Within a moment, Doreen was hugging her and the tears flowed from Doreen's eyes as well. There was the sound of a car arriving as Sharon's parents returned. I remembered her telling me that they were so worried that she was building her hopes too high and that she would be so disappointed; but Sharon had instead insisted that she was going to be healed. I simply could not resist it. I went to the car to find two very anxious people. With as sombre a face as I could manage, I said to her mother, "I think you'd better come and help her."

"Oh dear, is she so disappointed?" asked her mother as she leapt out of the car.

Still with a straight face, I said, "Well, you know how it is."

She went into the studio and there was her daughter, who, having stopped crying for a while, seeing her mother, burst forth once again. I have never known tears to reflect such happiness. Her father was still in the car, so I went to fetch him without telling him what had happened. He came into the studio and realising that the 'impossible' had taken place, went over to Sharon, (yes, there were tears in his eyes too,) and very gently he placed a hand on her shoulder and kissed her on the forehead.

I felt as though I was intruding on this very special occasion so I stepped back and thanked God for giving me the privilege of being there. The room was filled with a very special love. If only life could always be like that afternoon in March.

Sharon returned to work the next day and none of her friends had the courage to ask her what had happened. She could stand it no longer, and said, "Well, isn't anyone going to ask me what happened?"

With one voice they asked, "What happened?"

"I can hear. I've got two good ears like I said I would."

It was difficult for a bunch of hospital technicians to accept, so there was only one thing to do. She was taken into the Audio Department and given a full audio test. Sharon carries the test card in her handbag. It shows that she has full hearing in her right ear.

A few days later she kept her usual appointment with The London Hospital. Another full audio test and then a question, "Have you something to tell us?"

Sharon told them what had happened and they discharged her — after fifteen years.

Sharon had accepted her healing before she even came to Pin Mill. Her *expectancy* was the biggest contribution she could have made to her own healing. She told all her friends that she was going to be healed. That is really putting one's faith on the line! She told me that, as I prayed for His peace to be given to her, her mind seemed to be washed clean of all thought and a feeling of power rushed through her body. She then felt the power in her right ear — as though the deafness was being drawn out of her ear — and she was healed.

I have given this detailed account of the healing as it may be of interest to those who are more directly involved in this ministry. I also feel it to have been a very special time in which the love of Jesus Christ so filled the studio that, through Sharon's healing, we all received His touch.

The longer I am involved in the healing ministry, the less I am able to believe in coincidences.

More and more it becomes quite clear that these events are a part of God's almighty plan for us. The following is such an example of 'chance' events which led to the healing of a young boy.

Back Pains

This account of healing is told by a lady, Pam, who suffered from long standing back pains. It shows how a series of 'coincidences' led to the healing of a boy who was born deaf.

It all began in Nidri, a small Greek village on the island of Lefkas.

We shouldn't have been there at all! We were going to Turkey but something made us change our plans and choose Lefkas instead.

We *were* to have shared a villa with friends, but we found ourselves sharing the Villa Deglas with Jeff and Doreen. On the second day of the holiday we were out in a caique, sailing blissfully around the Ionian Sea. Somehow the vibration of the boat's engine had damaged my 'delicate' back. Next morning I couldn't move. My husband had to help me out of bed and help me back into it, and the pain grew during the next 48 hours.

Then Jeff asked, "Would you like me to do something about that back of yours?"

I accepted gratefully. We talked in that little villa by the sea for a long time, because I knew *nothing*, absolutely nothing about Christian healing. Our church does not have a healing group and all the years I had worked in a hospital, Christian healing had never been a part of my life's experience.

Then Jeff laid his hands, first on my head, praying aloud very simply; when his hands moved to my shoulders a tremendous heat moved into and through my spine and this was accompanied by such a tingling in my fingers as the pain gradually moved down and finally

out of my body. Finally, I was told to get up. I did...
easily and painlessly and, almost without thinking, I
touched my toes, sat down, got up, moved around. It
was incredible, even though I had never doubted that the
pain would go. Knowing what I now know, I think I
would have acted differently. As it was, I puzzled,
wondered and wandered around in what I can only
describe as a rosy glow of amazement, asking constantly,
"Why me? Why should I be so lucky?"

It was several days before I realised that the healing
with which I had been blessed went much, much deeper.
True, the dramatic pain brought on by the vibration of
the boat's engine had gone, and I felt 'different' in a way
which I could not then define. But gone too, was a long-
standing spinal problem. For thirty years I had suffered
from backache with pins and needles and neuralgia in
my right arm and fingers. I had had physiotherapy,
osteopathy, pain-killers and muscle relaxants, none of
which really worked. I had given up gardening, golf,
sewing and knitting and just had to 'get on with it'. At
the end of the first week in Nidri, all that pain and
discomfort had gone. I don't even know precisely when
it did go, so used had I become over the years, to waking
up each morning in acute pain.

Doreen and Jeff began to tell us more and more about
Christian healing, and one evening they told us of the
healing of Sharon's deafness. We were very moved by it
and somehow got around to telling them about Alastair,
our eldest grandson, now twelve; how he had been born
deaf, and was fitted with hearing aids at the age of three,
and a year or so later had gone as a boarder to the
Winston Churchill School for Deaf Children.

Born deaf
Somehow Sharon's healing kept coming to mind; we
asked about her, about her work, about her parents and

64

we as

On   lic   I knew I had to do
some   lenly. "Do you think
you

Jeff   ly, "I thought you'd
neve

So   n... and we prayed...
and   air to Pin Mill. We
didn   unknown which is so
com   't want to complicate
thing   cult. We didn't know
wha   im nothing.

W   Alastair played all
mor   eff. He hitched and
unhitched the tractor, going all round the garden on it,
with Jeff behind, shouting instructions. We stood on the
sideline, watching a lovely relationship being built up.
Later, Jeff took Alastair into the studio and explained
how the power of God can heal people, but he was
obliged to bargain with him. He traded fifteen minutes
on the tractor for fifteen minutes on the couch. Alastair
receiving the laying on of hands, and received his
'reward'... the tractor... and so it went on. When we
came back from our walk, I was asked into the studio to
persuade this lively little boy to keep still and receive a
further laying on of hands, at the end of which, Jeff
spoke to him and he answered without hearing aids. I
was amazed, and said, "He's hearing you!"

"Isn't that what we asked for?" Jeff replied.

At our next visit, Alastair's hearing improved further
after the laying on of hands and Jeff made a tape of their
conversation, carried out without hearing aids or lip-
reading. Later, Alastair picked up a speech tape from the
rack, looked at the title and asked if he might listen to it,
just with the ordinary head set with no hearing aids. The
joy and wonderment on his face is something I will

Thursday

August

14

I WILL INSTRUCT YOU AND TEACH YOU IN THE WAY YOU SHOULD GO.

Psalm 32. 8. (N.I.V.)

Home Evangelism

never forget and we knew, without doubt, that one day Alastair will have full hearing.

Next time Alastair's father went to Pin Mill and on that day the volume was turned down on the hearing aids.

On the next visit we took our daughter-in-law with Alastair and it was explained to her what was happening in the healing of his deafness. On our way back to school in Brighton, that evening, Alastair heard Sharon's story on tape in the car, against traffic noises, with one broken hearing aid and with a flat battery on the other side. He heard it all and was very interested. He had had a good day. Was it just the tractor which made him say he was 'happy *and* glad'? I don't think so.

Last week was special. We met Sharon. Alastair was intrigued as she told him how she had been healed of fifteen years of deafness.

It isn't his fault that his little mind is full of doubts. All his schooldays he has been taught self-awareness and encouraged to be realistic about his disability. "Deaf boys can't be Tristar pilots or Sea Link captains," he says without a vestige of self-pity... "but we must listen and think". I believe he is beginning to do both, in the way we want him to, so that he can be taught, slowly and gently, to become, like Sharon was, trusting and confident and ready. So that is Alastair's story... the first part of it... his hearing has improved. We know that we have the prayers and support of many people, for which heartfelt thanks. We know that we must keep faith, patiently, trusting that what we ask for we shall receive in the fullness of time... then I shall write the last part of Alastair's story.

*For **not** going to Turkey and for **not** taking our allotted villa we are very thankful. For having met Jeff and Doreen, for having sat above the engine of the*

66

caique in Greek waters, and wrecking my back, we must be so thankful, too, for it was surely meant to be that Alastair should be led to Pin Mill.

Pam

The Emergency

It is all very well to talk about counselling and discussion before giving the laying on of hands, but what happens in the case of an emergency?

Let us now look at two cases in which something had to be done quickly for the sake of the sick person.

Migraine

We had a telephone call at 8.30 one morning. The man gave his name and said, "I need help." From the tone of his voice it was plain that he was greatly distressed. I asked him what the problem was and he told me he had a very bad migraine. He lived locally and knew where we lived so I asked if he would like to come right away.

A friend brought him by car and as they arrived the man was holding his head in his hands. His eyes were shut. As he slowly got out of the car I led him into the studio.

It was immediately clear that this was no time for talking. I asked him his Christian name. It was Michael (that was not his real name). As he lay on the couch he sobbed and his whole body trembled with the pain. I placed my hands gently on his head and speaking very quietly, said, "I give this healing to you, Michael, in the name of our Lord Jesus Christ."

I then found myself saying, "Lord, I ask that you forgive Michael all his sins, and through your great love and compassion, release him from this pain."

Having given up this brief prayer I told him that he would feel the pain being drawn from him and into my fingers. His body was still trembling and he was still sobbing. I then asked him to tell me when the pain began to ease.

After some three minutes he told me that the pain was easing and, after another couple of minutes, he said that the pain had gone. I said, "Thank you, Lord." So did Michael.

He was still trembling when he got off the couch and sat in front of the fire. As I went to get him a mug of coffee, I suggested to his friend, who was still sitting in his car, that he should go and join him. He found it difficult to believe that Michael was out of pain.

While we sipped our coffee they told me that the migraine had started at 5 o'clock that morning. No amount of Pethadine had been able to relieve the pain, so his GP had suggested he came to see me. Then the questions started. Where did the power come from? Did healing happen every time I laid hands on someone? What was the power that came through my hands?

By this time Michael was nearly asleep as the drugs took over. So, in answer to their questions, I suggested that if Michael wanted to know more about his healing he should phone me and come and see me again. And they went on their way.

I wondered — would he come back?

The following day a very lively voice on the phone asked if he could return to Pin Mill and discuss what had happened the day before when his worst ever migraine had been healed in the shortest ever time.

Healings such as this support my belief that the physical healing acts as the sign that leads to the wonder of the spiritual healing to follow.

Strokes

It was another early morning telephone call. George gave us the distressing news that his wife, Gwyneth, an active member of our healing team, had had a severe stroke and was in Ipswich Hospital.

We knew that, if we were to help her, we had to get to her as soon as possible. She was deeply unconscious and the hospital staff had told us not to build our hopes too high as she was seriously ill.

That afternoon George, his son and daughter, the minister of their church and I, met at her bedside. Gwyneth was lying on her side with a tube down her throat. I told the sister that we were going to lay on hands and would like to draw the curtains around the bed. She was happy about this and told us to go ahead. George sat at one side of the bed holding Gwyneth's hand. The other three stood in silence while I positioned myself on the other side of the bed to lay hands on Gwyneth's head.

There was always the possibility that, although she was not conscious, her unconscious mind could absorb that which her ears would receive. I first said, "Gwyneth, this is Jeff. I am going to lay hands on you." Being aware of her strong faith, and having laid on hands many times herself, I added, "And *you* know what *that* means."

As I placed my hands on her head I was reminded of the four who brought their paralysed friend to Jesus and how He healed him by forgiving him his sins. I said, "Lord, we are reminded of the way in which you healed the paralysed man when his friends brought him to you. You simply forgave him all his sins and he rose and went to his home. Lord, we bring to you our friend, Gwyneth, asking that you forgive her all her sins, that she may be given new life — healed in spirit, mind and body to continue her work in your service."

I remained with my hands on her head for a few minutes until a nurse came through the curtain to see what was going on. Someone, bursting with curiosity, invariably does! I finished by saying, "Lord, we ask for this healing in your name."

As we prepared to leave, I turned to Gwyneth and said, "We want you back tomorrow, Gwyneth."

Later that evening, George phoned the hospital to ask how his wife was. He was told that there had been a slight flickering of the eyelids and a little movement of the lips. He was also told that he must realise she was seriously ill and not to build his hopes too high.

Next morning George phoned again to ask after Gwyneth. The reply was something like this, "We don't know quite how to tell you what has happened, but your wife is sitting up in bed and drinking cups of tea." She had been unconscious for twenty-four hours and the doctors were mystified. They had no explanation for what had happened and said it could only be described as a 'miraculous recovery' for they had never seen anything like this before.

Gwyneth told them that she knew what had happened. When they asked her to explain, she told them that she had had the laying on of hands.

A scan showed no damage to her brain, so she was given two lumbar punctures to check for other causes, but this found nothing. Eventually a small clot was discovered in her right leg. After a few days Gwyneth was allowed to make the journey to the bathroom by herself. The small clot caused a certain amount of discomfort but Gwyneth was discharged from the hospital and returned to her home.

Today, ten months after having the stroke, Gwyneth is about to start driving her car once again.

One of the doctors on the ward told me that it was a complete mystery that there was no sign of bleeding in her brain. As her case notes mention that she had the laying on of hands, I asked him if that might not explain why there was no bleeding. This he could not accept. And so, for the staff at the hospital, the healing of Gwyneth's stroke remains a 'complete mystery', ...except, that is, for a certain nurse who witnessed the loving, healing power of Jesus Christ and whose faith, like that of those who were also privileged to be there, is all the stronger for the experience.

Believing... the Key to Wholeness

I was invited to talk to a group of about twelve people in the rectory of one of our local parish churches. The subject under discussion was to be the ministry of Christian healing.

On similar occasions in the past, I have found it helpful, as I have said before, to take with me someone who has been healed by the laying on of hands. It gives those present an opportunity to question them directly about their experience, which is so much more convincing than if I try to relate events second hand.

I took with me Sharon, of whose healing you have read, and Ken, whose right arm, as you will recall, was to have been amputated because of the excruciating pain caused by ten years of cancer.

As I discussed some of the individual healings, I was able to hand over to my two companions. Sharon told how she had been left completely deaf in her right ear, and how she just knew, without any doubt whatsoever, that she would be healed if she received the laying on of hands.

Ken told of his healing. He told of the terrible pain from which he had had no relief during the ten years of his illness and how his arm was to have been amputated. He told of the vision of the man in the white robe, and how He stood beside him with a 'big stick' in His hand and how His head was all lit up. And he told how, at that moment, the pain left him and within three weeks the tumour was no more.

Questions were asked, discussion took place. They believed the truths that were spoken by my two friends.

When the rector first spoke to me about this meeting, he asked if I would give the address during the morning service on the following Sunday, five days later. He now asked if I would base my address on the subject of the rectory meeting, including the healing of Sharon and Ken.

After the service a number of people spoke to me of their interest in the healing ministry and accepted what I had been saying, while other comments can best be summed up by one man who said, "I found what you said of interest, but as you were speaking I was getting hot under the collar. If only — oh, if only I could believe that what you told us about the healing of those two people was true."

At the meeting in the rectory, people *met* Sharon and Ken, they *talked* to them and they were able to *touch* them, and they *believed the truth* of what had happened to them. Just five days later, the same truth was told to people in the church, but because they could not see them, touch or talk to them, there were those who, in spite of the medical evidence, found it so very difficult to believe in the healing of these two people. But those at the rectory meeting found no difficulty at all.

This experience has caused me to think of the way in which many of us have similar problems in believing what Jesus told us, that is not just paying lip-service to acknowledging His words, but really believing that He wanted us to accept and believe what He said. Otherwise He would not have bothered to say these things.

Take, for example, the crowds who gathered outside the house of Simon and Andrew in Capernaum. They were there because they knew that Jesus was in the house. They also knew that they could be healed by His word or His touch. There could have been little doubt in their minds, because they knew that this man, whom they could see, hear and touch, had healed many others. Had any one of us been there in that crowd, we too would have had no problem with believing. In fact we, too, may well have known people who had been healed by Jesus.

But when Jesus promised us that, whenever we ask, He will be in our midst, (Matthew 18:1–20), do we *really* believe Him, even though His presence may be in a different form, a form we do not understand?

Moreover, when He told us that if we have faith in Him we will do what He had been doing... and that whatever we ask in His name He will give to us, (John 14:12 – 14) do we really believe these words of Jesus? And if not, what sort of Christians can we call ourselves?

Today, when we attend a healing service or a fellowship healing meeting, we are in a similar position to those in the church who found it so difficult to believe that which was the truth, simply because they had not seen, spoken with and touched the two who had been healed. Yet it was the same truth told on the Sunday as was told earlier in the week when there was no difficulty in believing. It is the same truth, we are asked to believe today, as it was when Jesus walked among the sick in Capernaum. But because we cannot see a physical presence, the truth becomes difficult to accept.

Surely this goes some small way towards answering that unanswerable question, "Why are some healed and not others?" If we, who offer ourselves to be used by Jesus in His continuing ministry of healing, are unable to believe His word and do not really *expect* Him to keep His promise to those who ask Him for help, He must surely find it most difficult to work through such unbelieving channels. And if those who come to Him asking for help, do not really *expect* to receive it, the difficulty they may experience in accepting that which He is offering them, must be just as obvious. Whatever the outcome, let us not hear it said, "It is God's will that I should not be healed." God's will is for wholeness for all His children and when we ask for healing, we ask for the wholeness of spirit, mind and body. Sometimes we receive the healing instantly; sometimes it is within days, weeks and even months of receiving the laying on of hands. Seldom have I found that a healing prayer has resulted in no benefit at all.

But take heart, you who have difficulty in believing that your sickness and suffering can be healed. Know that the belief of friends, loved ones and those who minister, can be sufficient faith through which Jesus can heal you, just as the faith of the four friends who took the man, sick of the palsy, to Jesus, was sufficient for him to be healed... "When Jesus saw their faith, He said unto the sick of the palsy, Son, thy sins be forgiven thee. .. I say unto thee, Arise, take up thy bed, and go thy way into thine house" (Mark 2.1–12).

Perhaps, then, one of the most important prayers in healing is, "Lord, I believe. Help, Thou, mine unbelief." And when we do receive our healing, it is not enough simply to say, "Thank you, Lord. Goodbye for now, I'll come back if I have further trouble."

Our search for wholeness is an on-going 'self mission' for which one life-time is insufficient. If ever we are to come close to finding that wholeness, it can only be through constant obedience to the will of God. In addition to believing and expecting in our search for that wholeness, prayer and Christian fellowship are essential.

When someone is desperately ill, it is not always easy for them to believe in a healing, merciful God — particularly when they are in pain and feeling more ill than ever before *and* doubting whether it was wise to have agreed to chemotherapy in the first place. It is unlikely that those who are suffering to such a degree are capable of praying for themselves. They welcome the suggestion that they should not even try to think, but just to listen to the prayer of the one offering them the ministry, to relax, feel the warmth of the healing touch and surrender themselves into the arms of Jesus, the Healer.

The Mind of the One who lays on Hands

Now we have to examine our own thoughts as we are about to lay hands on the sick person. Let me tell you how I approach those cases for whom the medical profession hold out little hope.

First, I establish firmly in my mind, (sometimes speaking aloud for the benefit of the patient), that the power of God knows no limits. If our God is the God who created the universe, then the problem of this sick person which I am bringing to Him is, by comparison, very small. There can be no doubt whatsoever that if God can create this beautiful planet Earth, He is certainly capable of creating a state of wholeness within the body of this sick person.

At this point I concentrate my mind on Jesus and ask Him to empty me of all that is of me, and fill me with all that is of Him.

I am comforted by the fact that even Peter, James and John allowed their belief to falter and were, therefore, unable to heal the epileptic boy (Matt. 71:14−20). If it was sometimes difficult for them to believe, it is surely understandable that we, too, sometimes find it difficult.

Next, I remind the sick person that Jesus made a promise to be with us, and that, with faith in Him, we shall be able to do the things He did, and even greater things.

I confess to finding it difficult to believe that we will do even greater things than Jesus did! After all, He raised the dead. But why should I doubt even this promise? Maybe my faith is being stretched a bit too far, but I have no difficulty in believing that, if we have absolute belief and trust in Jesus, we will, at least, do some of the things that He did. I know this to be true because of the healing of Charles, who was waiting to have his cataracts removed. He did have them 'removed' and regained his sight by the touch of the healing Christ, *instantly*... Russell, who was blind and regained his sight, *instantly*... Ken, having had an incurable cancer in his arm for ten years, saw Jesus standing beside him and was healed, *instantly*... Sharon, deaf, and by placing a finger in her ear and asking for the power to open her ears, she was given perfect hearing, *instantly*.

There is no doubt whatsoever in my mind that these healings, and many more, were the work of Jesus, doing exactly as He promised. Being with His Father, He is in a unique position to intercede on our behalf. The writer of Hebrews (7: 24−25) tells us that, "Jesus lives on for

75

ever... and so he is able, now and always, to save those who come to God through Him, because He lives for ever to plead with God for them." He hears our healing prayer and, to bring glory to the Father, He gives the healing power of the Spirit to the sick person, using *our* faith and *our* hands.

There have been many more "instant" healings — bad backs, headaches, arthritis, phobias and allergies. The fact is that, when we talk about healings, we tend to dwell upon the spectacular healings and ignore the little ones. This I find disturbing (and I am guilty of it myself). All healings are the work of God through His Son and no one healing is more wonderful than another.

It must again be made quite clear, however, that not all healings take place instantly. The value of talking about the instant healings is that it gives convincing evidence to those who find it difficult to believe in a power beyond that of man. Many doctors, having a medical/scientific training, find it especially difficult to believe. But God is already working through the doctors, the surgeons and the nurses. Medicine is God's way of working through science and the laws of nature. Healing through the laying on of hands is God healing the sick person in spirit, mind and body without the intervention of man. But since God is in both, great benefit to the patient can be gained by one form of healing complementing the other. But it has been the healings that I have just mentioned that have opened the minds of the doctors and the doors of the hospitals to us and resulted in consultants sending their patients for Christian healing.

At a conference on Christian healing at which I had been speaking, someone asked me the usual question: "You have been talking about your successes, what about your failures?"

It is a question which, as I have already said, presupposes that the power and ability to heal belongs to the one who lays on hands, when, of course, nothing is further from the truth. If that question is to be asked, it should be directed to

Jesus, the Healer. In fact, just as we give thanks to Jesus for the healings that do take place, so we should seek guidance from Him on those occasions when complete healing does not take place as we expect it to. It is by listening to that small, quiet voice within that we can be guided to the cause of the sickness and to the block that may be preventing healing. On so many occasions healing does take place, but not in the way we expect it to happen.

But I shall deal with that important question in depth in Chapter 11.

Chapter 7

THE UNCONSCIOUS MIND IN HEALING

It is sad that the full potential within the human body to heal itself is seldom realised. In God's wonderful creation of the spirit, mind and body He has equipped us with the means by which we can assist our own healing in a way that is beyond medical science. In spite of this, in so many cases, we tend to ignore it.

Thousands of people are going through life in a constant state of panic, anxiety, phobia, physical illness and continual stress. In the majority of such cases their doctors are, perhaps understandably, mystified. They prescribe the faithful tranquilliser or try a new drug just on the market. If the prescription gives benefit to the patient, then more often than not, it becomes a case of "Keep taking the tablets".

I say that this is 'sad' because most of these people have, within their creation, the God-given ability to deal with many of these situations themselves.

Let me make myself clear. I am not pointing an accusing finger at the overworked GP. As one told me, "I can give no more than ten minutes to any individual patient in surgery, knowing that there is a waiting room full, all with their own individual problems, and I have to see them all before I commence my rounds."

If I am to be critical of anyone, it is of society in general because it has chosen to misunderstand or completely ignore the way in which the mind of the individual can be responsible for illness and how that same mind can be used to heal that illness.

The cause of this misunderstanding is a prejudice which

has surrounded the name given to a perfectly natural, God-given state of mind. A state known as 'hypnosis'.

Dr John Carey, MRCP, a General Practitioner, comments on the use of hypnosis in helping his patients overcome problems of this nature:

> During my work as a General Practitioner I occasionally have cases where the appropriate source of help is difficult to find. Many of these problem cases are psychological, and although the psychiatric services can sometimes offer help, patients may find that unacceptable, especially early on in their condition.
>
> Phobia or fear of things such as heights or crowded streets, is an example of the type of problem. A phobia may not appear terribly important or necessarily that distressing, but left without help can develop into a more complex problem and, in some cases, a bizarre behaviour pattern may occur. For instance, to avoid a distressing situation a patient may collapse complaining of chest pain, possibly wrongly convincing the medical profession of a heart condition, thereby camouflaging the phobia completely. It is, therefore, important to treat such cases at an early stage, certainly if an irreversible situation is to be avoided. On many occasions I have referred such patients to Mr Jefferies who has successfully treated them with the aid of hypnosis, thereby avoiding the use of unnecessary and possibly addictive drugs.

There will probably be those who say, "This seems to be departing from the simple model and teaching set by Jesus in the New Testament". To them I say, "Since those days, 2,000 years ago, God has given mankind the blessing of ever increasing knowledge with which we can fight disease and sickness. So, for God's sake, let us use that which He gives us in abundance, together with that which He taught us through His Son — and be grateful".

Let me return for a moment to those prejudices and misunderstandings. One cause has been the way in which hypnosis has been used in the name of entertainment. Stage hypnosis which involves members of the audience can leave highly suggestible people in a disturbed state of mind. The performing hypnotist has insufficient control over the individual to ensure that there is no lingering influence. Laws were passed forbidding public performances. But this has not prevented them from taking place at private functions. Recently there has been talk of changing such law and allowing local authorities to decide whether such performances may take place in their respective areas.

What then are these misunderstandings that colour public opinion in such a way as to ignore one of the most effective natural therapies being used more and more in major hospitals throughout the land?

Fact and Fiction

Let me attempt to clear some of the objections which are caused mainly by irresponsible theatrical performances and ill-informed comment.

No. 1 It is not right that anyone should allow their mind to be taken over by someone else.

The mind of the subject is not 'taken over' by the therapist (therapist is a less emotive word than hypnotist). The subject will remember everything that is said and happens while under hypnosis. In my own case I discuss fully what we plan to do and to achieve and only proceed with his or her full agreement. If people wanted to, they could quite easily prevent themselves going into hypnosis, simply by concentrating on something quite different. It has to be understood that it is the subject who, by his or her own ability, achieves this beneficial state of mind. The role of the therapist is to teach that person how to achieve it and to lead, when necessary, to an understanding of whatever problem they may have.

In the majority of cases I teach people to go into hypnosis by themselves. They can then use this new-found gift in their own home and deal with the everyday stress problems without drugs. And in such cases there is certainly no one else present to 'take over' their mind. They are in complete control of themselves. As I write, I have just received a letter from a lady who had been addicted to several different drugs to reduce high blood pressure which had been brought on mainly by stress and tension. I taught her how to relax in hypnosis and, in that relaxed state of mind, to pray for her healing.

She writes...

I am most grateful to you for teaching me your method of relaxation and prayer.

Having come off beta blockers by the start of the year, I have continued without them. It has been a busy year which, as well as its enjoyments, has brought strains and stresses, some in coping with the enjoyments! At these times prayer in relaxation helped me enormously, bringing calm and confidence.

So I hope that it is now quite clear that, while the therapist may guide the subject in the same way that a counsellor does, the mind of the subject is not 'taken over'. Indeed, when someone is using self-hypnosis, there is no one else present to even guide them, let alone 'take over' their mind. They are, in fact, in full control of their own mind.

No. 2 Hypnosis is dangerous and could harm the subject.

I know of no case in which hypnosis, in itself, has harmed anyone. The manner in which it may be used is, however, a different matter. If it is deliberately misused by some evil-minded person who, having gained the confidence of the subject, deliberately sets out to create a state of stress and trauma in that person's mind, then, of course, it could do harm. In such a case it could be rightly claimed that hypnosis is dangerous. But so would a scalpel be dangerous in the wrong hands. We have to assume that we are dealing with competent practitioners — genuine, sincere people who are committed to the care and healing of others, and place our trust in them, just as we place our trust in the pilot of the plane or driver of the bus in which we are a passenger.

No. 3 Am I going to tell the most intimate secrets of my soul and remember nothing about it when it is all over?

The subject will not talk about any event in life or discuss any subject that they would not wish to discuss in a normal state of consciousness. In hypnosis, however, the subject is able to call to mind events of the past that would not be possible in the normal state of consciousness. In such cases it depends wholly upon the experience and skill of the therapist, just as it would be had the subject been in a normal conscious state. If I ask someone in hypnosis to tell me about an event in their life which they have regarded as too personal to discuss, they will probably say that they do not wish to talk about it. In such event I ask why they do not wish to talk about it, and by talking around the 'personal' event, it is possible to discover whether it is something which requires further discussion when the subject is out of hypnosis.

No. 4 Suppose I do not come out of the hypnotic state when I am told to.

On the many hundreds of occasions that I have used hypnosis, I have never had anyone who did not respond to the instruction to open their eyes and be 'fully awake'.
I have, however, had occasion to induce a deep hypnotic state in terminally ill people who have been in severe pain

and desperate for sleep. In such cases they simply drift into a state of normal, peaceful sleep and awaken in the normal manner.

No. 5 In a state of hypnosis one is open to attack by evil spirits.

There are those who, understanding even less than the average ill-informed critic of hypnosis, throw their hands in the air in horror, claiming that evil influences can enter a person while in hypnosis. If any evil influence was going to enter the mind of the subject it would be more likely to do so during a general anaesthetic when no part of the brain is within the control of the patient and could, in such circumstances, be said to be "open to attack" — or even during normal sleep, when that person, although being aware of the dream taking place in the unconscious mind, has no control over what may be going into or being taken from the mind. An incompetent therapist, on the other hand, can leave a patient with a troubled mind, one they did not have before therapy. But that is an entirely different matter and nothing for which hypnosis can be blamed.

The Mind in Healing

Let us now look a little more closely at what happens in hypnosis.

Of the many books I have read on this subject, few agree on the manner in which hypnosis is explained. Some go into great detail concerning left brain and right brain function, which I am sure is of interest to the medical profession, but of little real assistance in the application of hypnosis in Christian healing.

It must first be appreciated that someone in hypnosis is in a state of acute awareness of everything that is taking place around them. So much so that it is sometimes difficult to convince the subject that they have been in a state of hypnosis. Again, the popular misconception is that one is totally blanked out and that, upon coming out of this state, the subject has no memory of what has taken place. Far from this, it is my experience that, unless told otherwise, a person coming out of hypnosis is able to give a far more accurate and detailed account of what has taken place than someone who has been in a normal state of consciousness. It is true to say that hypnosis can better be described as a state of 'super-consciousness', as demonstrated by some of the following cases. Indeed, on a scale which ranges from a state of coma at the lower end to hypnosis at the top, the normal conscious state is said to be somewhere about half way between the two.

For those of us involved in the ministry of Christian healing, it is only necessary, when using hypnosis, to have a mental picture of what is taking place in the mind of the subject. It is vital that, when laying on hands, we are given the complete attention of the sick person, and that their mind should not wander off onto the material problems of everyday life. Peter and John found this when they approached the "man lame from his mother's womb", at the gate of the temple (Acts 3:1−8). The man's mind was concentrated on attracting the attention of those passing into the temple so that they might give him money. Peter and John knew that if they were going to be able to help him, they first had to get his whole, undivided attention. "And Peter, fastening his eyes upon him with John, said, 'Look on us'. And he gave heed unto them, expecting to receive something from them." The man's mind was now given wholly to the two men before him, and he *expected* something to be given to him — and he was given his healing. I am not suggesting that the man was hypnotised, but his attention was focussed on Peter and John in such a way that he might expect that which was to be given him.

Hypnosis, then, is one way in which the sick can direct their own mind onto the subject of their healing.

The ability to achieve this state of mind is already within everyone. It is just a matter of being able to discover it. It is rather like learning to ride a bicycle. Before doing so we are unaware of our latent ability to balance on those two thin wheels, but with a little help from a friend who may give us instruction, we find that we are able to balance without any difficulty. So it is with learning how to go into this very beneficial state of mind.

When we go to sleep at night we dream, and these dreams are often very vivid, and sometimes frightening. But we have no control over the events within these dreams which take place in the unconscious mind. In such a state of sleep our conscious mind is to a large extent 'switched off', leaving a small part to remain 'on guard' to respond to external influences; for example, when the alarm bell rings in the morning to wake us. And sometimes, at the point of waking, what has been happening in the unconscious mind is transferred to the conscious mind as we come into a fully awakened state — and we can recall our dream.

At that point when our conscious mind begins to wake up and first becomes aware of what is happening in the unconscious, we are, for a fleeting moment, in a state of hypnosis. The same applies when we go into a state of sleep. As our conscious mind winds down, so we become aware of our unconscious mind. In hypnosis it is the state of overlap with which we are concerned, a state in which both conscious and unconscious minds are within the control of the subject.

It has to be agreed that what I have just described concerning sleep and dreaming, is a perfectly natural state of the mind and something that we have all experienced. Hypnosis is merely the control of this natural state of mind. Whereas in natural sleep the conscious mind is largely 'switched off' and unable to control events within the dream, in hypnosis it is relaxed to a far lesser degree and able to control the activities of the unconscious mind. In this state, just as when we remember our dreams, the conscious mind is able to witness everything that is taking place in the unconscious and take complete control of whatever may be happening.

As every event in our lives, since the time of our birth, is stored in the unconscious mind, it will now be seen how those who have a troubled mind can be helped to examine these events and discover what may be causing the dis-ease within them. When an unhappy event occurs in our life we try to forget it. All we are doing is suppressing the memory of it — like burying a fused bomb. In later years we receive a jolt in life and the bomb starts to tick away resulting in sickness.

In hypnosis we simply enter the unconscious mind, locate the bomb, examine it and defuse it. In this way we heal the cause rather than mistakenly attempting to overcome the problem by trying to heal the symptom.

Before anyone can be introduced to the benefits of hypnosis, complete confidence has to exist between the subject and the therapist. If the subject takes an instant dislike to the counsellor/therapist or does not feel at ease and comfortable talking with and confiding in him, then, there is no point in continuing. In short, the subject has to find the counsellor an acceptable person if he, or she, is going to receive help.

It will, I hope, be of encouragement to the reader to learn of some of the ways in which I have used hypnosis together with the laying on of hands in the healing of 'incurable' conditions.

Heal the Mind — Heal the Body

Dorothy (not her real name), a young mother of some 32 years, had been a very keen long distance runner but, unfortunately, she had developed arthritis in her knees. No longer could she enjoy her favourite sport. The doctors advised her that surgery to her knees would free her from the pain and she would be able to run once again.

Dorothy had surgery to both knees and the result was said to be satisfactory — except that she could not run. She could walk and she could walk fast but, as much as she wanted to, she could not run.

An X-ray examination of her knees showed that there was nothing wrong and the surgeon told her that there was no reason why she should not be able to run. He then suggested that she should have some physiotherapy and for six years Dorothy went to the hospital for treatment but there was no improvement in the condition. So it was that she came to Trinity Methodist Church asking for help.

She told the minister, Patrick McCluskey, of the problem. Her doctor had suggested that if there was nothing wrong with her knees, she probably had a mental block, and if that was the case there was little he could do to help her. It was agreed that this might well be so and I went to the church to meet Dorothy and to talk to her about Christian healing, at the same time explaining how the block, which she was told she had, could be removed. I explained how, with the opening of her mind to admit the healing power of Jesus, He would be able to remove the block and enable her to run. Then I put that important question, "Would you like me to do that?"

The answer came quickly, "Yes, please."

I showed her how she could be relaxed by my talking to her. I then told her that, in this relaxed state, she could visualise herself walking and running — but I explained that it would be necessary for her to come to Pin Mill where there was plenty of room to run about. After all, a church was hardly a suitable place in which to resume such an active sport as running!

When Dorothy came to Pin Mill she lay on the couch and went into this wonderful, relaxed state of hypnosis. I sat at the head of the couch, placed my hands on her head and prayed aloud for the healing of her spirit, her mind from which we asked the block to be removed and for the healing of her body.

By talking to her she was then able to visualise being outside the studio, in the garden. Again, I must make it quite clear that visualising in this way, was actually like being in the garden. It was as real as the most vivid dream. She could hear my voice all the time, at first suggesting that she should walk around the garden and this she did, at the same time describing what she saw in some detail. Next I told her that she could walk around the garden again, this time, if she wished to, she could break into a run. She told me what she was doing, "I'm walking. I'm walking fast. I'm walking faster — and faster. Now I'm running. I'm running. I'm running fast.".

Dorothy told me when she had 'returned' to the studio — still, of course, lying on the couch. I then rejoiced with her that our prayers had been answered and the block removed. With this thought well in her mind and the experience of having just run around the garden, I asked her if she would like to do it *again*. This was a most important word — *again*. It established in Dorothy's mind that, having already run in the garden, there was nothing to prevent her from doing so *again*.

I told Dorothy that she could open her eyes and get off the couch. She went into the garden and started to walk. Her pace quickened — just as it did in her unconscious mind when lying on the couch. Then she broke into a run. When she arrived back at the studio door she was out of breath and explained "I'm a bit out of condition!"

Back in the studio, she lay down on the couch once again and I laid hands on her giving thanks for her healing. After six years of treating the body with no results — just thirty minutes of healing the mind and Dorothy's troubles were over.

Heal the Memory — Heal the Sickness

I recall Jenny (not her real name), a young lady of 22 years being sent to me by her doctor. She was a very attractive girl, smartly dressed and altogether a pleasant personality. Whenever her boy friend asked her out for a meal, whether it was at a pub, restaurant or a private party in someone's home, she would begin to feel sick. If they continued and actually attended the party or attempted to eat in the restaurant, she would have to leave the table and retire to the ladies' room and vomit. Her doctor had tried everything that was likely to 'settle' her stomach in an attempt to avoid this unpleasant behaviour. But still it persisted.

When she came to me I asked her to tell me all about her problem and I learned that she had never experienced this feeling of sickness in her own home, where she lived with her mother and father. So far as she could remember she had had this trouble since she was about eleven. I suggested to her that we should try to discover the first occasion when it happened, together with the event which had been responsible for her feeling sick whenever she was about to eat anywhere other than in her own home. With this knowledge we could set about healing the cause and the symptom would no longer exist. She agreed.

Jenny was an excellent subject and I was able to take her back to her childhood. She went back to her tenth year and by asking a few simple questions it became quite clear that, at that age, she had no problems with eating — wherever she might be. So we looked in on her eleventh year and I told her to go straight to the occasion when she first experienced the feeling of sickness when eating away from home. Jenny was able to tell me that she was at her aunt's house where she was staying on holiday for a week without her parents. She told me that it was pancake day, and they were having lunch — she, her aunt and her cousin, a boy a few years older than Jenny. She had been given one pancake and, after

89

a bit of a struggle, she had managed to get that down. Then her well-meaning aunt insisted that Jenny would like another pancake. There was no way she could get another morsel past her lips. The very thought of it made her retch. Sitting at that table was rapidly becoming a torture — and this was only the first day of her holiday.

I took Jenny to the following day and the same problem arose. The very thought of eating made her feel sick. To attempt to eat while feeling like this would be courting disaster.

We now had a simple explanation for her sickness at the age of eleven. This was the first time she had been away from home by herself. She came from a happy home life where she was a much loved child. Quite simply, Jenny was 'homesick'. While she was still in hypnosis, I explained this to her and made her understand that her feeling of sickness was nothing to do with eating; it was to do with missing her 'mummy and daddy'. I went on to tell her that nearly all little boys and girls become homesick when they leave home for the first time.

I told Jenny that she would remember feeling homesick and I wanted her to come forward to the present time at twenty-two years of age. I told her that as she came forward, she would leave all feelings of homesickness behind in her childhood. This she did. I asked her if she remembered feeling homesick when she was a little girl. She said that she did. I then told her that young women of twenty-two do not feel homesick; they leave all that behind them in their childhood. She agreed that this was so. I told her that what had been making her feel sick when she was about to eat away from home, was the memory of a little girl who did not like leaving her parents — a long time ago — and all this was now left in the distant past and would never worry her again.

To convince her that this was so, I asked her, still in hypnosis, if she would like to go out for dinner with her boy friend. They arrived at the restaurant of a pub called 'The Bull' where they had a large, three course dinner. All the time she was eating I was commenting on how much she was enjoying it and how different it was from those days when she was a little girl staying at her aunt's house. I finished by telling her that it would always be like this in future — no more worry about sickness because all this was left far behind in her childhood.

Jenny had no more problems with sickness when dining away from home.

Heal the Mind — Heal the Speech

Peter (not his real name), a man in his late forties, came to me with a problem he had had all his life. He had a bad stammer and could not remember being without it.

He worked in a large garden centre and was responsible for the propagation of the plants — a job which brought him in contact with the public and with suppliers. It was on these occasions that life became difficult for him. He found great difficulty in pronouncing his own name on the phone, and he had to make many phone calls each day.

Peter was a church organist, so it was not too difficult to talk to him about the Christian attitude towards healing. This was clearly a case for hypnosis, so I explained what I was about to do to ensure that he was happy about it.

He went into hypnosis and was able to visualise going into a small chapel where he was seated in front of a cross. At this point I prayed for his tongue to be untied and that he would be able to speak without hesitation. I spoke to him and he answered me without the slightest stammer.

I recorded the session so that he could hear himself afterwards, speaking without the stammer he had struggled with for as long as he could remember.

When he came out of hypnosis he was still speaking without the stammer and asked if I would help him to speak on the phone without the usual hesitation. So he went back into hypnosis and visualised himself sitting at the desk in his office. He picked up the phone and made two or three phone calls and was surprised to find that there was no problem.

The next thing that occupied his mind was a lecture he had been asked to give on the propagation of plants at Essex University in two months' time. So once again he used the power of his own mind, in hypnosis, and visualised being at the university, speaking to an audience of five hundred people (far more than would have been there on the day). The talk he gave was most interesting. I found myself listening to him and allowing him to continue far longer than was necessary!

When we had finished, he said "It was very strange seeing all the difficult words coming up and being able to speak them without difficulty."

Some months later I had a letter from him in which he told me that the lecture had been a great success. He had enjoyed speaking so much that he over-ran his time and the chairman had to ask him to finish. His own mind had been the instrument through which our Lord had untied his tongue and he was no longer a prisoner of the spoken word.

The complexities of the human creation are well beyond the total understanding of man. We should not be surprised, therefore, if we find that we cannot always arrive at a clearly defined approach to healing which alone can effect the wholeness we pray for.

As in orthodox medicine, it is sometimes a combination of drugs and surgery followed by physiotherapy — and very often 'trial and error' treatment — that provides the effective solution. There are occasions when this is so with healing. Sometimes by prayer and the laying on of hands alone, a healing will take place. At other times we need to call upon the natural, God-given resources of the sick person to assist in their healing. We have already discussed how hypnosis can relax the mind and body and we have seen how the power of the mind can enable someone to visualise through the powerful imagery of the unconscious mind. When these are used during the laying on of hands, the ability to receive divine healing is greatly increased.

Psoriasis

Elizabeth (not her real name), a young mother of a one year old girl, came to me asking for help with the healing of extensive psoriasis which she had had since she was eleven. For the past sixteen years she had been receiving treatment from the hospital, where she was working at that time, without any sign of improvement. This is no reflection upon the hospital, because psoriasis is a most difficult and obstinate condition. They had been trying to overcome the problem by giving ultra-violet treatment and liberal applications of creams.

Elizabeth wore her hair long and in a manner that would cover the psoriasis on her forehead, ears and neck. The psoriasis was not on her legs or arms but was extensively over the remainder of her body.

She told me that she had decided not to continue with the hospital treatment — at least for a while — and on the advice of a colleague in the hospital, Elizabeth came to see me.

I am convinced that psoriasis is caused by the mind, and that it can be healed by the mind. Having said that, we have a great deal more to learn about the way in which the mind can be used in the healing of this distressing condition.

It was necessary to discover when the condition was first noticed and learn something of the cause of its onset. To do this I simply taught her how to relax and go back in her life to the period a few months before she first noticed the sores on her skin.

Once we had discovered the cause of the psoriasis, the memory of which was still deep in her unconscious mind, we could heal that memory (cause) through prayer. This would be followed by the laying on of hands for the healing of the condition of her skin, which was the symptom of the cause.

It was not long before we found it.

Elizabeth loved school and the subject she enjoyed more than any other was clay modelling. Sadly the teacher, a man, for reasons we do not understand, on a number of occasions made Elizabeth sit still with her arms folded during the whole lesson when she was forbidden to touch the clay. He also had a habit of shouting at her which frightened her. It was a few weeks after this first happened that Elizabeth began to show signs of the skin disorder which was to dominate her life during the next sixteen years.

I dealt with the healing of this unhappy memory by laying on hands while she was visualising the schoolroom situation and taking away the fear of the teacher. I explained that hers was the very natural reaction of a little girl, but when she grows up the fear will have left her, as "grown-up ladies are not afraid of school teachers". We also forgave the teacher for being unkind to Elizabeth.

During discussion about other events in her life, I learned that her first pregnancy had resulted in a still-birth. The distress of this had caused the psoriasis to take a violent turn for the worse, and when she became pregnant for the second time, the memory of the still-birth was with her and the anxiety resulted in a greatly worsened condition. When she became pregnant the hospital could give her no further treatment as this would have put the life of the unborn child in danger.

A beautiful, healthy baby girl was born to Elizabeth, but the psoriasis was still very much with her. When she breast fed the baby the pain was intense. The baby was nearly one year old and Elizabeth was still suffering from the sores which covered the greater part of the front and back of her body.

We discussed the manner in which we would give the healing. To begin with I would relax her and give her the opportunity to visualise her healing taking place. Then I would lay my hands on her head and say a prayer for her healing, after which I would ask that she be filled with God's healing power. I told her that she would experience this as a warm, tingling feeling throughout her whole body. When she told me that she could feel this power, I would place my hands on the affected areas and she would feel a build up of the heat and the tingling sensation. After a short while the feeling would fade and this would be the sign to us that the healing was finished on that particular spot for that session.

In agreeing all this with Elizabeth, I asked her to imagine that the heat she would feel was the opening up of all the pores of her skin and that the tingling was the new skin forming beneath the sores.

It was important that I should have her agreement to, and understanding of, all that we were about to do. It was also important that she felt my hand directly upon those parts of her body that had for so long been responsible for the distress and sadness in her life and which, on so many occasions, had been the cause of people, who did not understand the condition, keeping their distance and giving her a feeling of being rejected.

After our first session, Elizabeth told me how much she wanted another child and mentioned the warning given to her by the hospital. I explained that if she was no longer going to the hospital for treatment there was no reason why she should not become pregnant; there was nothing in what I was doing that could possibly harm the unborn child.

Two months later she arrived for healing with the news that she was pregnant. There was great rejoicing. I am mentioning this because throughout the following nine months, during which Elizabeth came to me regularly for healing, the psoriasis gradually, but most definitely, cleared from her body.

About three weeks before the baby was due I asked the consultant dermatologist at the hospital if he would like to see her. He examined her, particularly on her scalp and behind her ears where there was not a sign of psoriasis. he turned to me and said, "I'm impressed. What did you do?"

Before I could tell him, he referred to her pregnant state and added, "I couldn't have touched her in that condition."

He pressed the question, "Will you show me what you did?" So we showed him.

What happened next was equally important. Elizabeth had a beautiful baby boy and during one of her visits to the post-natal clinic, a small black mole was found on her right thigh. She was advised to go to the hospital and have it checked which she did, and was told it was a skin cancer. She was a blonde with the usual fair skin which offered little protection against the years of ultra-violet treatment. It is safe to assume that this treatment had, at least, been partly respons-ible for this skin cancer. It was cut away there and then. But the damage was done. The word 'cancer' was all that was needed to create a further state of stress in her mind... and back came the psoriasis.

The first thing needed was to reassure her that this did not mean that she was about to get cancer in other parts of her body. Try as I might, I could not convince her. It took the consultant, with the authority and credence we, the lay public, invest in the medical profession, to finally sweep all doubts from her mind. But did it?

We continued with the healing as before, but the psoriasis showed little signs of change.

Elizabeth suggested that we leave the healing for a while and come back to it fresh in a month or two.

This we did. When I next saw her the psoriasis was almost as bad as it had ever been. We prayed and laid on hands as she relaxed and visualised the healing taking place. Another appointment was made for the following week.

Elizabeth arrived for healing, and with hardly a word, lifted her hair from her forehead. A week ago it was covered in psoriasis, from hair line to her eyebrows. In just seven days it was clear!

She was thrilled and I was delighted. We both knew that this change could only be in answer to our prayers. After a few more weekly visits Elizabeth was completely clear of the psoriasis which had dominated her life since she was eleven.

My experience is that each attack becomes more difficult to heal than the previous one, but I am convinced that much more research should be carried out into the healing of skin disorders through the mind of the patient. A treatment that would carry with it no dangerous side effects whatsoever is much needed. If the mind can cause disease I am convinced that the same mind can heal.

Chapter 8

USING HYPNOSIS
IN CHRISTIAN HEALING

There may be those who, reading of the use of hypnosis within Christian healing, express concern over the ethics of this practice.

When I was first led to consider the use of hypnosis, it was to assist in the healing of a young man suffering from a 'terminal' brain tumour. I questioned whether this was a true Christian approach, so I prayed about it. I asked God to show me if this was acceptable in His sight. I then found myself 'hearing' that still, small voice within, saying, "Make your own judgement. If good comes from using it, then you can be sure that God is in it." Much good came from it. God was in it, and the young man was healed. Since then I have used it to great benefit whenever the need has arisen. I see the use of hypnosis as an additional therapy which, when used in the context of Christian healing, can help the sick on their journey towards wholeness.

As I said in the previous chapter, our ability to control the thought processes within our conscious and unconscious mind is a perfectly natural achievement. Just as we are able to 'switch off' our conscious mind and enter a state of sleep, so we are able to 'relax' our conscious mind and, when necessary, bring into awareness events stored within our unconscious. We are, in fact, learning to use our mind more fully. Since our mind is very much part of God's creation, when appropriate, we should use this gift, to assist in our healing. We do not think twice about praying for the healing of a sick person while, at the same time, giving drugs — and praying that the drugs will play their part in overcoming the sickness... and so we should. So why think twice about praying for the healing of the sick person while, at the same time, inviting them to use the power of their own mind in assisting their healing?

If, as I hope is the case, you will now be asking how one goes about using hypnosis within Christian healing in the manner I have described, the following will be of interest.

In Chapter 7 I described in some detail how, in hypnosis, the conscious mind is able to enter the unconscious to the benefit of the sick person. This, under the guidance of a therapist, can enable that person to bring into consciousness past events which have been the cause of a present sickness. The cause can then be healed by counselling together with prayer and the laying on of hands. There is however one more general use for hypnosis from which almost everyone, sick and healthy, can benefit and that is by relaxing in a way not possible by any other natural means.

I have evolved a straightforward procedure which, when used within Christian healing, can be a blessing to those who come in a state of mental and physical distress, asking for help.

Let us now look at a simple method of inducing this form of relaxation, and then we will look at the way in which a person can be taken back in their life to discover and heal unhappy, damaging memories.

I mentioned earlier that learning to go into hypnosis is rather like learning to ride a bicycle. The first time you make the effort is most important, because, if you fall off the bicycle at the first attempt, your confidence is likely to take a knock. If you have difficulty in going into hypnosis on the first occasion and are left with a feeling of failure, there is a possibility that you will approach the next attempt with that same feeling of failure. Once anyone has learned to 'ride a bicycle' — to go into hypnosis — they will never have a problem in achieving this state of mind on any future occasion.

First I ask the subject if he or she wishes to visit the bathroom. This is so important. If someone has travelled many miles to see you, it is possible that they need to attend to the call of nature — and you certainly will not get their undivided attention if they have their mind on their bladder the whole time. It is an obvious point but a most important one, I can assure you!

Having explained the benefits of hypnosis to the subject, explain what you are about to do, as follows:

Let us assume we are dealing with our friend, John, upon whom we laid hands in Chapter 5. We first decide whether he would like to relax in a comfortable armchair with a good headrest or to lie on a couch. Let him decide. If he has no preference, I suggest that, for the first time, he should lie on a couch. Explain to John that if he is going to use this form of relaxation at home, he will find it easier to lie on his bed, so the couch may be of greater help to him.

When he is lying down, tell him what you will be doing before you actually do it, and that he does not have to do or say anything, just enjoy the experience.

Tell him that you will show him how he can relax his body and then relax his mind. In the following induction I refer to 'the bright spot in the centre of the disc'. This can be anything from the back of a watch, to a coloured spot on a disc. It is simply a convenient spot upon which the subject may rest his gaze. Then explain what you are about to do, saying something like this:

> Your mind is governed to a great extent by what you see and what you hear. If you listen to what I am saying, that more or less takes care of what you hear, but every time you move your eyes a new image is registered in your brain and your concentration is disturbed. To help you concentrate, I am going to hold up this disc and I

want you to fix your gaze on the bright spot in the centre. Don't take your eyes from this spot. You can blink quite normally as you look at it and as you do so — and it will only happen when I say so — your eyes will start to get tired. You will find that every time you blink your eyes will become more and more tired. Your eyelids will become heavier and heavier until they become so difficult to keep open that they will close all by themselves. I don't want you to close them. They will close by themselves.

When they are tightly shut I will count you down from ten all the way down to one. As I go into lower and lower numbers, so you will go deeper and deeper into this wonderful state of relaxation. You will, in fact, be super-conscious.

I want you to lie with your arms and hands down by your side, and decide from this moment on, that you are not going to move your hands or arms. Try to make your body relax and become like a rag doll.

In a moment I am going to hold up the disc and I want you to keep your eyes on the spot in the centre of the disc. When I say so — and it will not happen before that — your eyes will start to become tired.

At this point the disc is held about 18 inches from John's head and a little 'above' the normal line of sight. This causes slight eye strain which hastens the 'tiredness' of the eyes and speeds the onset of the state of hypnosis. Then continue:

Your eyes will start to get tired... *now*. As you look at the spot, your eyes become more and more tired.

Every time you blink, your eyelids become heavier and heavier.

If, as sometimes happens, the subject develops a stare and does not blink, it is as well to comment that he should blink normally, and that he will find that every time he blinks, his eyelids will become heavier and heavier, and more and more tired.

> Every time you blink your eyes become more and more difficult to open, more and more difficult to keep open. Heavier and heavier...

It is the repetition of this suggestion of eye-tiredness which brings about the state of tiredness in John's mind and soon he finds that it becomes impossible to keep his eyes open any longer.

As you are talking to John, watch his eyes. You will be looking for the signs which tell you he is responding to your suggestions. When he blinks, his eyelids open a little less with each successive blink. When you see this, confirm...

> Your eyes are becoming more and more tired... heavier and heavier...

When the eyelids are opening about half the normal amount, say to him...

> In a moment you are going to blink and your eyes will remain closed ...heavier and heavier ...tighter and tighter ...tightly shut, tightly shut. So very tight... and you cannot open them. Tightly shut.

It would not be advisable, on the first occasion, to challenge anyone to open their eyes. If they were able to do so, it would destroy their confidence in future attempts — and the important thing during this first session is that they should build confidence in themselves and in the therapist. Continue as follows:

> I am now going to count you down from ten all the way down to one, and as I go into lower and lower numbers, so you will go deeper and deeper into this very pleasant state of relaxation... Ten, nine, eight ...going down, deeper and deeper, seven, six ...more and more

pleasant, five, four ...so very peaceful, three, two and one. Well done! You have now achieved that peaceful state of mind known as hypnosis. You have done very well!

Now, as I promised, I am going to count from one to five. When I get to four your eyes will open and on five you will be back to your normal conscious state.

I stress that healing should be enjoyed. In our search for wholeness, we are coming closer to God, and that, surely, must fill us with hope and joy.

Now that John has discovered how to relax in this way, you ask if he would like you to lay on hands and pray for his healing. He will almost certainly ask you to do this, in which case you simply hold up the disc once again, ask him to set his eyes on the spot and talk to him as I have already explained. When he is relaxed in hypnosis, lay hands on his head and give healing in the normal manner. Because he is so relaxed and without tension, he is able to absorb the prayers and receive the healing so much more effectively.

There is hardly an illness or condition that does not bring with it a state of tension. What I have just described is, without doubt, the most effective way of reducing tension and, most important, without drugs. Guiding someone into a state of hypnosis is quite simple and straightforward. It is at this point that they can be helped in so many ways.

Let us assume that John suffers from claustrophobia and has great difficulty in travelling by train to his place of work every morning. When he eventually arrives, he is always in a distressed state and if, as often happens, he has to attend a management meeting at the beginning of the day, he develops a state of extreme anxiety. This causes him to develop psoriasis on his arms and hands (this is typical of many cases).

With John in hypnosis, we have laid hands on his head and prayed for the healing of his spirit, mind and body. We then ask, in prayer, for his mind to be released from the fear of being in confined spaces.

Having completed this prayer, come round and sit beside John, so that you can watch his face and note his expression as the healing of his mind takes place. You then say to him:

> I am going to count from one to five and when I get to five you will be on the platform waiting for your train to take you to work in the morning. The platform will be crowded and I want you to tell me what you see around you. Will you do that for me?

It is most important that John realises that he always has a choice. He will almost certainly agree to do as you have asked.

Having counted from one to five, add straight away:

> You are there on the platform. It is early morning and the platform is crowded with people on their way to work. In a moment the train will arrive. I want you to tell me when it is pulling into the station.

When John tells you that the train is arriving you tell him:

> This morning you are going to get on the train without fear. We have prayed to Jesus Christ asking that the fear be taken from you. So, when you step onto the train I want you to shout aloud, "Jesus Christ is with me and all is well." No one will hear you. All fear will leave you and you will find that you actually enjoy the journey.

It is important that you are able to visualise the situation into which you have placed John. Ask him to let you know when the train pulls out of the station and when it is pulling into the next one. Then tell him:

> At the next station more people will get onto the train and it will be more crowded than ever before, but it will

not bother you at all. You will be saying to yourself, "Jesus Christ is with me and all is well," and all fear will have left you. You will be so happy.

The next step is to take him to his office, where by the same positive approach, he is able to attend his morning meeting, without stress, and enjoy his day.

This done it is made clear to John that every morning, from this day forward, when he gets onto the train he will say quietly, within himself:

"Jesus Christ is with me and all is well."

Before he is brought out of hypnosis, you will say to him:

Now that, through Jesus Christ, you have overcome all fear of travelling on the train or any other confined form of transport, you no longer suffer from stress. Because you no longer suffer from stress, there is no longer any reason for the psoriasis to develop on your arms and hands. So let us give thanks for your healing and lay hands on your arms and hands that they may be healed.

What we have just dealt with is visualising as in a dream. Now we are going to deal with another problem which John has. For as long as he can remember, he has always been terrified of dogs, big dogs and small dogs. It is a great embarrassment to him. Whenever he visits friends with dogs, no matter how timid they may be, John comes out in a cold sweat and begins to tremble. Since John has had this problem for as long as he can remember, we have no particular time or age to which we can refer.

One thing we can be sure of is that the memory of the cause of the trouble is stored deep in his unconscious mind — just as every other event in his life is stored in his unconscious. What we have to do is take him back to this event and heal the memory of it.

It would be possible to tell him, as before, that you will count from one to five, and on five he will be confronted with the cause of his problem. This, I suggest, would be a most abrupt and traumatic confrontation which should be ruled out. First you tell him what you are about to do and get his approval to your suggestion. Then do it.

I have devised the following gentle way in which to heal the memory of early years. With John pleasantly relaxed in hypnosis, say to him:

> I am going to count from one to five. When I get to five you will be in a white room. It has white walls and in the wall facing you will be a blue door. Would you like to do that?

When John tells you that he is happy about your suggestion, you count from one to five, and on the count of five say:

> You are in the white room. You are in the white room with white walls all around you. In the wall facing you is a blue door — a brightly painted blue door. Tell me when you see the blue door.

We are about to take John gently back in his life and before each step we seek his approval.

When John tells you that he can see the blue door, tell him to go over to it but not to open it. When he tells you he is by the door, ask him which side of the door the handle is on. You are doing this to find out how quickly he responds to your question and with what degree of certainty he replies. Whether he says left or right, you say:

> Good, that is absolutely correct.

This is to give him confidence that he is doing well. You now tell John:

> I want you to open the door and go through. You will

106

find yourself in a corridor which goes to the left and to the right. I want you to turn left and look down the corridor. Will you do that?

With John's approval you continue by asking him to shut the blue door behind him. Then:

As you look down the corridor you will see that in the right hand wall of the corridor are many open doorways. Over the first doorway is a number. That number is your present age. Over the next doorway is another number — your age last year; and so the numbers appear over all the doorways right down to the one marked nought.

When John says he can see these doorways, you can set about finding when the event took place which resulted in his present fears. Let us assume that it took place after his fifth birthday. In this event if he went back to his fourth year, he should have no fear of dogs. Say to him:

I want you to walk down the corridor until you come to the doorway numbered four. Would you like to do that? Tell me when you get to that doorway.

When he is at doorway number four, tell him to look through the opening and he will see a small boy. Ask him to tell you when he sees the boy. Then ask him what the boy is doing and describe the clothes he is wearing. This will tell you the extent to which he is 'seeing' the boy. Next, say to John:

That little boy is you when you were four years old. If you go through the doorway you will be four years of age. Would you like to do that?

If John says that he does not want to go through the doorway, there will be a good reason. Possibly the reason is that he is aware of the event that caused his fear of dogs. If he does wish to go through and does so, ask him to tell you when he is through. Then ask him how old he is, and he will tell you that he is four years old. From this point on you have to bring a dog into the visualisation and see how he reacts. If he shows no fear, you ask him to come back into the corridor and walk up to the next doorway, number five. Go through the same procedure and discover how he reacts to dogs.

When he eventually enters the year of the unhappy experience, by counting from one to five will take him to the original encounter which caused the trouble. How you deal with the situation from this point onwards depends upon the nature of the encounter. It is probably sufficient to explain that most little boys are afraid of dogs and are not always aware that the dogs just want to play. But when those boys become adults, they have no fear of dogs because they leave that fear behind with their childhood.

When the reason for the fear has been explained, ask John to come back into the corridor and back to the blue door. When he arrives at the blue door ask him to open it and go into the white room, shutting the door behind him. Tell him that this time there will be a comfortable armchair in the room and he is to sit in the chair. Having done this say that you are now going to lay hands on him and pray that all the fears remain with the child of five. Now, in his adult years, there is no fear of dogs — in fact he will now find that he is rather fond of dogs. Tell him that waiting on the other side of the blue door is a large dog that is anxious to make friends with him. Ask him if he will open the door and greet the dog in a friendly manner, telling him that all fear of dogs was allowed to remain with the little boy of five. When he opens the door you can control the actions of the dog by telling John what breed the dog is and how it will behave. Ask John to pat the dog and talk to it. Tell him that this proves that not only is he now unafraid of dogs, but dogs like him.

Finally, you bring him out of hypnosis telling him that from now on all is well. At this point it confirms the healing if John is put in contact with a friendly dog when he can repeat that which he did in hypnosis.

We now come to showing John how he can help himself to overcome these problems by simply relaxing in self-hypnosis.

When John is thoroughly familiar with the verbal induction, it can be explained to him that if he lies on the couch and fixes his gaze on the spot on the disc which you will hold above him, he will go into hypnosis by himself. All he has to do is to say to himself, quietly, in his mind only, the things that you had said to him:

> I am going to look at the spot on the disc and when I say so my eyes will start to get tired. They will start to get tired *now*. More and more tired. Every time I blink my eyes will become more and more tired. Heavier and heavier, etc.

When he has achieved a state of hypnosis you tell him that in future, he will be able to spend as much time as he wishes, relaxing in this way. But now, you will remind him what he has to do to bring himself out of this pleasant state:

> When you are ready to finish your relaxation exercise, simply count from one to five, quietly, within yourself. On four, your eyes will open and on five you will be back to your normal conscious state and very happy.

It is important that we assume a responsible attitude towards those who come to us for help in this way, so when I am dealing with someone who is a car driver, during their first session in hypnosis, I tell them:

> You will go into hypnosis only when you are here with me, or in your own home when you plan to do so. Do you understand that?

Then I repeat this statement because I have in mind those who may have a vivid imagination, and develop a fear of going into a hypnotic state while driving a car. But by dealing with it in this way, any such thoughts are prevented from entering their mind.

Beyond this point it must be left to the individual therapist to develop his own approaches. He should use hypnosis in the context of healing prayer. God has blessed us with the ability to use our minds in this way and it is through prayer that the therapist is guided towards an effective healing approach.

Chapter 9

A JOURNEY INTO WHOLENESS

Extreme pain in knees and ankles. She had to be carried from car to studio. (She was left with me while her father went for a walk down by the river.) I had to lift her from one chair to another. Explained healing and lifted her onto the couch. I laid hands on her head and prayed aloud. Laid hands on knees. She felt warmth. She normally felt no pain when sitting or lying down, only when standing or attempting to walk. During the laying on of hands on her knees, they twitched. I asked if they had done that before. She said they had not. She then stood up. There was no pain. She walked across the studio to me... sobbed and laughed, saying, "I haven't been able to do this for months!" We hugged each other and said, "Praise the Lord! Amen."

So read the first set of many notes made during the following year.

Jane (not her real name), had a most horrific skin disease known as psoriatic arthropathy. Large areas of her body were covered in suppurating scabs. The nails on her fingers and toes had developed into what looked like little lumps of cement. She had a severe form of psoriasis which associated with arthritis and the pain in her limbs was such that she was confined to a wheelchair. She had been in this state for some months, during which time she was being treated by the hospital as an out-patient. Jane was just 18 years old.

That immediate response to healing prayer, when she got up and walked for the first time in months was, for me, a positive sign that Jane was going to be healed. When we had finished celebrating and giving thanks, she walked, unaided, back to the car where her father was waiting for her. It was an event her father often recalls as one he will never forget.

It was during the previous Sunday evening when we held one of our regular healing services at Trinity Methodist Church that Jane came asking to be healed. The service had finished and some of the people were leaving; others were standing around chatting. From the back of the church came a young girl, partly walking, partly being carried by her boyfriend. She staggered into a chair and was obviously in great pain. Unfortunately I had another appointment and could not spend time with her. I explained why I could not stay but told her that I had good news for her. I said, "The power of God can heal you, and that's good news, isn't it?"

I told her that, if someone could bring her to Pin Mill, I would be able to spend whatever time was necessary and lay hands on her. We arranged that she should come to the cottage on the following Sunday morning.

And so Jane started out on her long journey in search of wholeness.

Jane had little faith, but she came asking for help — hoping. Orthodox medical treatment had produced no results. Her body was in such a state that the consultant dermatologist at the hospital insisted that she be admitted. I had mixed feelings about this because it meant that we were unable to continue with the healing that had only just started. On the other hand I realised that unless she had immediate care and attention, those terrible sores on her body could become septic.

Jane was in hospital for six weeks during which time I visited her and learned that the treatment she was receiving was a liberal application of cream over the whole of her body, while, to deal with the pain in her joints, she was given a regular supply of pain-killing drugs.

When the cream had done its job and the scabs had been

softened away, arrangements were made for Jane to spend time in a special skin clinic in Israel. She was there for a further four weeks, soaking up Israel's warm sunshine and the healing ultra-violet rays. Then she returned to the UK when she had planned to continue her schooling.

Jane had been back from Israel for three days when I had a phone call from her. "Hello, I'm back," she said, "but so is the psoriasis."

She had been back in this country for just three days when the dreaded sores began to reform all over her body.

"Can I come and see you?"

During the weeks that followed I was able to see her almost every other day.

Driving her home after one of our healing sessions she asked, "Why has God given me this terrible disease?"

I explained that God had not given it to her. I said: "You were born a beautiful baby. Sometimes something occurs in our lives that causes bad things to happen to us — like sickness."

I went on to say that in many cases of cancer we find that there has been some traumatic experience in the person's life that triggered off the cancer. I further explained that once we discover what that trigger experience is, we can set about healing the memory of it.

"How do you find out what experience has caused the sickness?" she asked.

"I teach people to use their conscious and unconscious minds by going into hypnosis. When people can do this, they are able to start putting their lives in order."

Immediately she asked, "Can you do this for me, so that we can discover what caused my psoriasis?"

I told her that we could and should. Jane could not wait to start.

It was a few days later that Jane came to Pin Mill. She lay on the couch in the studio and went into hypnosis. She was a remarkably good subject and was able to visualise vividly, but on this occasion, she was going back into her past to discover what happened in her life just before the first attack of psoriasis when she was twelve years old. By talking to her I led her into the room as I had done with John, in which there were white walls around her and in the wall facing her was a blue door. She then opened the door and went into a corridor which had a number of open doorways down the right hand side. Over the first doorway was a number. That number was her present age. Over the next doorway was a number — her age the previous year... and so the doorways were numbered, right down to her first birthday.

I said, "I want you to walk down the corridor until you come to the doorway with the number eleven over it. Tell me when you get there."

After a few seconds Jane told me that she had arrived at the door numbered eleven. I said, "If you look through the doorway you will see a small girl. Tell me when you see her."

When she told me that she could see her, I explained that the girl was herself at the age of eleven and I asked her to tell me what the girl was wearing.

I received a sharp answer to that question, "She's wearing that horrible green school uniform!"

Jane went through the doorway and became the eleven-year-old schoolgirl. In fact, she was simply reliving the memory of a day at school which occurred seven years previously. She told me that she was in her class-room.

This was the point at which I could start to find out exactly when the psoriasis started and, most important, what caused it. I next asked her to go to her room, take off her stockings and jumper, look at her legs and arms and tell me if she could see any marks or sores on her skin. She did this and told me that her skin was perfectly clear.

I then asked her to come back through the doorway, into the corridor and walk up to the door numbered twelve. When she looked through this doorway she saw herself at twelve years of age. She was wearing a pair of dungarees.

She said, "She's not very happy." I asked her to go through the doorway and this she readily did. Now I was able to ask her why she was not a happy girl.

"I can't say."

By the tone of her voice I could tell that she was becoming disturbed. So, very gently I continued to ask why she was unable to tell me what had made her so unhappy, and eventually she said, "The man told me not to."

At this point I had a pretty good idea what had happened to her, but I had to be sure, so I continued to ask her. "Do you want to tell me about it?"

Jane began to sob and was becoming more distressed. It was necessary to discover something of the nature of what the man had done to her that had caused such growing distress.

In a faltering, sobbing voice, she said, "He told me that he was going to help me with my lessons."

"And did he help you with your lessons?"

"No."

"What did he do?"

There was no reply.

Jane became very distressed. "He started touching me," she said.

"Where did he touch you?"

There was no reply. She just expressed her feelings in the sounds of distress for which no words could be found.

By now it was painfully obvious that I was dealing with a case of child abuse.

She told me what had happened and who the man was.

At this point I decided that I had enough information with which to talk to Jane in her normal conscious state and explain to her how this most unhappy experience could be the cause of all her psoriasis. I told her that, although she would remember everything that had just happened, she would feel no trauma, no distress, and that we would be able to talk about it calmly.

When she came out of hypnosis, she was no longer distressed. We sat down and talked about it and she told me how the man had removed her clothing and fondled her. Within two months her whole body was covered in the most horrific sores. Months of medical treatment finally gave her relief and she was clear.

Jane had already told me that she had had a second attack of psoriasis when she was fifteen. I suggested that we should use hypnosis to discover the cause of this but she said, "There's no need to, I now know what caused it."

She explained that a similar, but more serious incident occurred and within two months she was once again covered in psoriasis. This attack was worse than the previous one, and, once again, she had to undergo months of treatment in this country and abroad before there was any sign of relief.

With this information it became quite clear that the nature of her relationship with her boy-friend was responsible for this, her third attack of psoriasis.

Jane confessed and there were no longer any secrets. We could now set about healing Jane in spirit, mind and body.

Raising her Spirits

At 18 years of age, Jane was confined to a wheelchair for much of her day and when she attempted to walk, it was with two sticks. So her enthusiasm for life had taken a bit of a knock and her spirits were at a very low ebb.

It is my belief that Christ's healing power is more readily received when the mind of the patient is filled with positive thoughts. Negative thoughts lower spirits and act as a block to the healing power of Jesus. I remembered a young woman who had cancer of the liver saying to me, "I don't think I could ever cope with being well again." There would have been no point in laying hands on her and praying for the

116

healing of her body when she was in that state of mind.

Jane had been inactive for so long and all her school friends had left her as they pursued their further education and were planning their careers. Months of hospital treatment and the isolation which this condition forces upon the sufferer had dulled Jane's enthusiasm for life and sapped her energy to fight on until she was well again.

During one of our healing sessions I asked her what she most wanted to do when she was well again. She did not hesitate. "I want to make a parachute jump and I want to learn to fly a plane."

This was good news. I explained that she could take advantage of her newly discovered ability to use her unconscious mind and do both without delay.

The experience of visualising these events stimulated her mind. She talked excitedly about them and said that she wanted to do them again for real when she was well enough. In a similar manner, she visualised going to a sunny island in the Pacific Ocean, where she swam and sunbathed and refreshed her mind once again.

It was the beginning of April and although Jane's mental condition was brighter her physical condition was still very serious. The important information which had been revealed concerning the cause of her illness was not known to the consultant. I persuaded her to let me speak to him as it was important that he should know the facts.

When I told him what I knew, he simply put his hands to his face and asked me to tell him everything. He decided immediately that we should work closely together for the healing of Jane and asked if I would come with her for the appointment that afternoon.

He examined Jane and then asked me and her father, who had brought her to the hospital, to join them for a talk. The first thing he commented upon was Jane's attitude to life. She was now thinking more positively and he told us that he would like me to see her as regularly and as often as I could find the time to do so. We decided upon a healing session every other day. During this time a relationship of complete trust grew between us. Without this, I doubt very much whether Jane would have been healed.

Psoriasis, although not a killer disease, can completely wreck a person's life. The bright red patches of scaly skin, sometimes, as in the case of Jane, thick masses of scabs, the discomfort ranging from extreme itching to excruciating arthritic pain in the joints, affects thousands of people in this country. Yet, to get an appointment to see a consultant on the National Health Service, sometimes means waiting for up to six months or more. It is with this in mind that I am giving a detailed account of Jane's healing. It is just possible that her suffering and the patient way in which she received her healing may be of help to others.

So what did we do?

Healing of Psoriatic Arthropathy

At the beginning of every session, we had a prayer for the healing of Jane's spirit, mind and body. However, at the first healing we prayed for the forgiveness of the men who had abused her and which had caused the long months of suffering. She would then go into hypnosis so that she could visualise her healing actually taking place. As I laid my hands upon her and could feel the power being given to her, I would then suggest that we concentrated on one particular part of her body. The worst affected parts of her body were her legs and feet, particularly her feet. Her arms, hands, ears and scalp were also in a very bad state. The psoriasis extended beyond her hair line and onto her forehead. We would, for example, concentrate upon one of her arms and hands, and I would lay my hands on that arm and tell her that the arm would begin to increase in heat until she could only just bear it.

When it was as 'hot' as she could comfortably tolerate, I

explained that what she was feeling was the healing heat opening up all the pores of her skin and now her skin was able to breath properly. I would then tell her that she would begin to feel a tingling sensation together with the heat in her arm, and that the tingling sensation was caused by all the beautiful new skin forming beneath the scabs. Soon she would find the new skin coming to the surface as all the bad, old skin fell away. It is important to make quite clear that all this took place within much prayer and that the old skin going and the new skin forming were in direct answer to those prayers. Because of the suggestions given to Jane, her mind was able to accept that her healing was actually taking place which, indeed, it was.

By June we were beginning to see the difference in Jane's skin. They had noticed the change at her home. Her walking was also showing improvement. The consultant told us that Jane's state of mind and her general attitude was due wholly to what we were doing at Pin Mill.

Jesus — Yesterday and Today

During these days together I was able to talk to Jane about some of the healings that Jesus worked, and we studied the events surrounding the healing of Simon's mother-in-law in some detail. I told her that had she, Jane, been there in Capernaum in the days when Jesus was there, He could have laid His hands on her and she would have been healed immediately. I further explained that it is the same Jesus who heals us today, but today we cannot see Him. Then a thought occurred to me. I remembered an occasion during evening prayers at a conference organised by The Churches' Council for Health and Healing. We were in that beautiful chapel of the Divine Healing Mission at Crowhurst. Prayers were being led by my good friend, the Rev Ian Cowie. He asked us to close our eyes and meditate upon the scene in Capernaum when Jesus was walking along the hot, dusty road with James and John on their way to the house of Simon and Andrew. He continued with this story to the point where we may have been invited to join our Lord during the meal that followed.

As Ian was describing the events of this well-known story, I wondered just how many of us were able really to project ourselves into the situation that was being so graphically described... But if someone was led through a similar meditation — someone capable of using their unconscious mind, as when visualising in hypnosis — they would have an experience that could change their lives. They would, in fact, be opening their mind and inviting Jesus to enter it. They would 'see' Him and they would be helped in their unbelief.

With this in mind, I asked Jane if she would like to go to Capernaum and, perhaps, meet Jesus who could then lay His hands on her and heal her of the psoriasis. She welcomed the idea and was eager to start. First we read, once again, the account of this healing in the Gospels and, when we were as prepared as we would ever be, she went into this wonderful state of relaxation.

Drawing closer to Jesus

Jane found herself in Capernaum. She was dressed as a young Jewish girl wearing a white garment and a blue head shawl. On her feet she wore sandals. The first thing of which she was aware was the sudden heat. Crowds of people were around her and she was standing in front of a large temple. I asked her to go into the temple where she would find a number of people gathered around one man who was talking to them. When she was in the temple I asked her to make her way through the crowd and go to where the man was speaking. This done, I asked if she knew who the man was. She replied, in a voice which reflected a certain amount of surprise, "It's Jesus!"

Within a few moments a man who was shouting and

foaming at the mouth was brought to Jesus. Jane told me that the man became quiet as Jesus healed him and everyone was amazed.

Next, I asked Jane to go out of the temple and tell me when Jesus and his two friends, James and John, also came out. She did as I asked and told me that they were walking away from her as they made their way towards the house of Simon and Andrew. I said, "Why don't you go and walk with them?" With an understandable reserve, Jane replied, "Do you think they would mind?"

"No, of course not. You go and ask Jesus" I said.

She was quiet for a few moments so I asked her what was happening. "I'm walking between James and Jesus and Jesus is holding my hand."

Although I was just sitting beside her in the garden room, I began to feel as though I too, was with them as the four of them walked along that hot, dusty road on their way to the house where Simon's mother-in-law was waiting for them.

Once inside the house there was no sign of the lady, so I suggested to Jane that she went to the lady's bedroom where she might find her in bed with a fever. She found her lying on a low, hard bed with a single sheet over her and went to tell Jesus of the lady's condition. He came and healed her. The lady rose from her bed and, as Jane commented, "She seemed a little bewildered." So I suggested that she went with her and helped her prepare the food for the supper that was to follow.

As Jane took the food into the living area where Jesus was, I told her that He may well ask her if she would like to join them for the supper and sit at His table. I added, "Would you like that?"

"Oh, yes!"

Jesus did ask Jane to sit at His table. She told me that Jesus sat at the head of the table with James and John on either side, while she and the lady sat next to James and John.

As the meal progressed, she heard the sound of people gathering outside. Babies were crying, dogs barking, people shouting.

I said, "Jane, the people who are gathering outside are going to ask Jesus to heal them. Some of them will be blind, some deaf and many will be lame and there will be some who are suffering from psoriasis. Why don't you ask Jesus to heal you of your psoriasis before He goes out to all those people?"

Once again she asked, "Would it be alright?"

I reassured her and said, "He will lay His hands on your head and He will say: *Jane, your faith has made you whole.*"

I then asked her to let me know when Jesus placed His hands on her head, because at that point I would lay my hands on her head also.

Jane did as I suggested and Jesus laid His hands on her head. She was quiet, so I asked, "What is He saying?"

To my surprise she replied, "He's saying: *Have faith, Jane, and you will be healed.*"

I was surprised because this was not what I had told her He would say.

Until this moment Jane had taken all my suggestions and had responded faithfully to them. Suddenly I realised what was happening. It is at times like this that a little more of the truth is revealed to us, and all one's beliefs become that much stronger. I have always been sure that, in a way we shall never understand, Jesus is with us when we meet in His name. So He was with us during this visualisation and healing. Jesus, the Healer, knew that if He had spoken within Jane's mind the words I had given her, she would have come out of the experience, looked at her arms and legs and seen that the clusters of scabs were still there. Her faith would have been shattered and I dread to think what course her healing would have taken. Is it not conceivable that the Divine Healer who, through Jane's ability to 'see' Him, corrected my suggestion to Jane and gave her absolute reassurance that her healing was taking place and that, in time, she would be cleansed of this terrible skin disease?

After Jesus had laid His hands on Jane, He went outside the house where He was confronted by a large crowd of people. All of them were asking to be healed. Jane followed Jesus as He left the house to go among the people, together with James, John and the lady. At this point it seemed that I should end the encounter, so I suggested to Jane that it was time to come back and that she should say farewell to her friends.

After a few moments I asked her what was happening, "I've said goodbye to James and John and the lady."

I said, "What about Jesus?"

"Jesus is busy," Jane explained; but she did manage to make her way through the crowd to bid him farewell. And so Jane returned to her normal conscious state.

Fortunately I kept the tape recorder running, for Jane exploded, "That was the most fantastic experience of my whole life."

I asked her to tell me, in detail, everything she had experienced and she gave me a remarkable account of the events in the temple, the walk with Jesus to the house, the layout of the house, the events in the house, including her helping to prepare the food, and, of course, the time when she sat at our Lord's table and when He laid His hands on her and others who came to the house.

Jane said, "I'm no longer the same person!"

If any one of us had a dream of such a blessed happening during normal sleep, we, too, would surely have awakened a changed person.

Anything you ask in my Name

For those who need further proof of the presence of Jesus on these occasions, let me record what happened next.

Before going home, Jane asked if we could say a prayer

asking Jesus for her friends to make contact with her. For many months her friends had gone their various ways while Jane had been unable to join them in any social activities. She had simply lost touch. We said a simple prayer asking for them to make contact.

Two days later I arrived at Jane's house to collect her for healing. When she opened the door I was immediately struck by the change in her appearance. She looked happy and had a sparkle in her eyes. I noticed that the psoriasis on her face was considerably improved, but there was something else. When she got in the car she said, "Do you remember our prayer that my friends would contact me?"

I said that I did.

"Well, look what arrived in the post this morning."

She handed me a letter from one of her girl friends. When I read it I could only believe it was in direct response to that prayer which was given on July 8th. The letter is dated the 9th and it was received on the 10th when I collected Jane.

These are some of the passages from that letter:

Dear Jane,

I thought I would write you a letter as I haven't seen you for ages. I heard that you're feeling pretty fed-up at the moment. I know it may seem like it, perhaps, but we haven't forgotten you. We do miss you and I keep thinking about you. It's hard to say things through a letter, 'cos I don't know how you feel or if you'll think this sounds ridiculous, but I'm sure that if you can believe in God, He can help you. It is easy to discount the Bible as a load of rubbish, but what it says makes sense, and, although I feel lonely and cut off from everybody in it at times, I cannot forget the times we have really *known* there must be a God.

I don't want to keep on in case this sounds really glib and stupid to you and you'll think I'm a right wally, but too many people have found it to be true to reject it as something unreal and idealistic. There are promises throughout the Bible that God will help, so you have a right to claim them — otherwise God must be a liar, and He isn't!

Don't think I'm preaching to you, 'cos I don't mean it like that, but I know you were interested and, hopefully, still are. Also enclosed is a piece from a book which helped to reassure me, and still does.

We *are* thinking about you and praying for you.

Love, KC

The piece from the book, *One in the Spirit* by David Watson (Hodder and Stoughton), which was enclosed, reads as follows:

The Christian hope is not to be confused with blind optimism... Christian hope does not have its roots in the changing circumstances of life, in which hopes and dreams are often shattered and buried. Rather, it springs, first of all, from the deep conviction that God is the Lord of history. In spite of the vicissitudes of history and the enigmas and disappointments of life, He is leading His people to a glorious goal.

I find it impossible to believe that this letter was not in direct answer to our prayer, but it did not end there. On the day immediately after our prayer that Jane's friends would make contact with her, another friend, a hair stylist, called at the house. She said she knew Jane had not been able to get to a hairdresser for some time, so she had come to her to give her a new hair-style. To work on a head that was covered in psoriasis was not the most pleasant task, but the transformation in Jane, both in appearance and in spirits was a joy to see.

There is an interesting postscript to the story of the letter. About two years later, I met KC and I asked her if she remembered writing to Jane when she was ill. She did remember, so I asked what prompted her to write. She said, "I don't really know. I just had a sudden impulse to write to her." That requires no further comment from me!

It was the turning-point in Jane's healing. We continued with the laying on of hands until she was absolutely clear, just as she is today.

Why was it that Jane's prayers were answered so promptly and the healing of her psoriasis became so evident? Could it have been that, by Jane opening the doors of her mind to Jesus, she allowed Him to get closer to her than at any other time in her life?

Dr Leslie Weatherhead tells of a similar experience when a young woman came to him suffering from multiple sclerosis. He recalls it in *Psychology in Service of the Soul* (Epworth Press, 1929). The chapter is entitled, 'The religious value of hypnosis'.

> ...the patient was lying hypnotised on a couch, her headmistress (who had accompanied her) sitting at the patient's feet. I told the patient to dream that Jesus was standing by her side with a radiant smile on His face, that she looked up into His eyes and smiled, that He then bent down and touched both her legs. On saying this I laid my hands lightly on her thighs at the place she had indicated as being where she felt the disability most acutely. On being awakened, she sat up with her face transfigured. "I have seen Jesus," she said excitedly. "He touched my legs and I am sure I am going to be well." With this, she got off the couch, and, though she had come into my room that evening leaning on a stick on one side and on the arm of the headmistress on the other, she walked across my room without any help at all. Unfortunately even at the time of writing she is not healed, but she has never gone to where she was before this dream was suggested, and I am hopeful that, by

keeping up her expectation of recovery, her confidence, optimism, and high spirits, I can at any rate co-operate with the medical practitioner, so that his medical treatment may result in a more speedy recovery than would otherwise have been possible.

Some readers may feel that the patient was deluded about the presence of Christ. It is not easy to decide what actually happened. I should answer the objection by pointing out that it is no more a delusion than any other ordinary dream, that it was justified by its results, and that it is not impossible that one was allowed by the suggestion under hypnosis to open a door in the mind of the patient through which the Divine Friend, who is ever near us all, could pass into the inner sanctuary of the patient's life and there manifest His healing and radiant presence.

My copy of this book shows that there were no less than nineteen impressions printed between 1929 and 1946. And here we are in 1991, over sixty years later and there is still a great lack of understanding about hypnosis and the part that it can play in bringing us to that state of wholeness that must surely be the goal of every Christian. Hypnosis is a perfectly natural state of mind, given to us by God to be used for the benefit of mankind, yet in so many cases we would rather depend upon man-made drugs, many of which contain dangerous ingredients resulting in harmful side-effects and, in extreme cases, death.

Chapter 10

DEALING WITH CANCER

If there is one particular problem brought to the Fellowship more than any other, it is that of cancer. I would like then to share with the reader some of my experiences in dealing with cancer patients, their spouses and families. But first, I must make it quite clear, once again, that I have no medical training from which I draw conclusions — just experience in dealing with the many who have come to our Fellowship asking to be healed.

The stresses and tensions that can build up between members of the family and the one who is sick are both dangerous and damaging. All too often it takes the form of rejection of the spouse by the one who is ill. It is as though the cancer victim — particularly if he is a man — recognising that he is no longer the healthy, active, virile partner, feels that he can no longer fulfil his obligation within the partnership. With this in mind, he sets about finding a way to reject his wife before she rejects him. He often shows this rejection in the most callous way.

A couple had arrived at Pin Mill and were sitting in their car in the garden. The man had advanced cancer. He had been to see me several times before with his wife who acted as his chauffeur. As I approached the car I could see that his wife was crying. He sat motionless beside her in the front passenger seat and when I asked what the trouble was, she said, "He has just been telling me how very much he hates me."

I knew them to be a devoted couple, both highly intelligent, loving people. By having each of them in the

128

studio individually, I was able to talk with them and lay hands on them healing the rift between them. They left me with their arms around each other.

Many of those who come for healing are of the opinion that cancer is always a killer and this is the first negative attitude to be overcome. If no action is taken when cancer is diagnosed, then, of course, there will be little to prevent it from spreading to other parts of the body. Such neglect would almost certainly result in the death of the patient. On the other hand when the appropriate action is taken immediately, there is every opportunity for the disease to be beaten. I cannot stress too strongly that the healing I am describing should be complementary to orthodox treatment. This is a view strongly supported by Dr C R Wiltshire, MRCP, FRCP, a Consultant Clinical Oncologist:

> I have been involved in the care and treatment of people who have cancer for about 20 years. During that time I have seen a considerable number of changes in treatment, some of which have led to major advances in the likelihood of cure from this disease. Even where our ability to cure cancer has not been achieved, we now see a great improvement in the ability to palliate and to improve the quality of a person's remaining life.
>
> While major changes and improvements in the technology of medicine have happened over this period of time, there has, I fear, been a tendency to lose sight of the person 'as a whole'. The recognition of a need for greater objectivity in application of treatment and assessment of its results has sometimes led to a relative disregard of the less easily definable spiritual (in its widest sense) aspects of patient care.
>
> The past 10 years or so have seen a quiet, but consistent 'revolution' on the part of some patients with cancer who decided either to reject what they see as the brutality of modern orthodox medicine or at the very

least to complement it with other approaches to health-care. The recognition that people need more than the 'bricks and mortar' of care has therefore prompted many of us within the profession to give greater emphasis to the whole person in devising treatment policies. It has become clear to many of us that one of the prime needs of patients who have serious illness is that they need to maintain a sense of control over their destiny. The fact of the disease itself and the way in which treatment is often applied tends to remove any sense of an ability to self determine events. It is therefore not surprising that some individuals will seek approaches to healing which allow them a degree of autonomy.

We are just beginning to scratch the surface of what might be possible in the very diverse area of 'holistic' care and healing. There is much anecdotal evidence, but little consistent objective information to go on. Never-theless, I believe that, where appropriate, patients should be actively encouraged to seek complementary care whilst conventional treatment is being offered and especially when it is all too clear that conventional orthodox treatment has nothing to offer. The exact form of this type of 'adjunctive' care must of course be suited to the individual's own spiritual and cultural require-ments. Where possible, guidance should be given so that desperate patients and families avoid the more bizarre, expensive, and occasionally, frankly, disreputable 'alter-native' therapies presently being offered. In the longer term, I hope that the mutual acceptance of complementary care into orthodox medicine will lead to a greater ability to allow objective assessment of the results of applying such care. I believe it is necessary to do this (and as possible) as for any new treatment or drug.

In America, research has been carried out on a group of 86

women with breast cancer. In all cases the disease had spread to other parts of the body, so the chances of survival were not good. They were divided into two groups, both of which had standard orthodox treatment, but one group was taught to use self-hypnosis. The extension of life of the group which did not use hypnosis was on average 19 months, and after ten years none was alive. While those in the other group had an extension of life averaging 37 months and after ten years three of them were still alive (*The Lancet*, 14 October, 1989).

The report of this research states that the treatment (self-hypnosis) group were led by a psychiatrist or social worker with a therapist who had breast cancer in remission. It appears that their approach was to encourage the patients to discuss their doctors and to be more assertive with them. Also to support each other and overcome feelings of social isolation. "Thus groups countered the social alienation that often divides cancer patients from their well-meaning but anxious family and friends." ..."Emphasis was on living as fully as possible, improving communications with family members and doctors, facing and mastering fears about death and dying, and controlling pain and other symptoms."

There is no mention of a spiritual approach to the healing of the patients. If their state was improved without the help of Christian healing, I am prompted to suggest that even more may have survived had they devoted time to prayer and allowed the power of God to play a greater part.

There is so much evidence that the power of the mind can play a vital part in healing.

In America, once again, Lawrence LeShan has carried out a great deal of research into why some individuals get cancer and some do not — and why some are able to fight successfully for their lives while others succumb to the disease. As LeShan says in his book, *You can fight for your life* (Thorsons), cancer can kill but it can also be killed.

Visualisation

Having created within the mind of the cancer patient a degree of hope and understanding about the manner in which healing can be received, it is important that they are encouraged to use their powers of visualisation to assist in the destruction of the cancer cells. First, they are shown how to visualise being in a small room by themselves, standing in front of a full length mirror. The mirror is an 'X-ray mirror' which shows a normal reflection of their whole body with the exception of the ailing organ. This is shown as a coloured image of the uncovered, bare organ.

It can be explained to the patient that the job of the white cells in the blood is to circulate throughout the body and fight disease. So, when hands are laid on the spleen, which produces the white cells, the patient will be helped by visualising a heavy build-up of white cells around the spleen and in the area between the two hands. When the patient has visualised a sufficient build-up of white cells (they may be visualised as being rather similar to grains of rice), they can then be released to hunt down and destroy the cancer cells. The visualisation may be taken a stage further by 'seeing' the mass of white cells clustering around the tumour, wherever it may be in the body. Before they get there, the diseased part of the body is seen to be black, but as the white cells do their job, so the black becomes a healthy, bright pink.

On the next occasion when the patient receives healing, the tumour is seen to be not black as before, but a dark grey. As the laying on of hands is given, so the patient visualises the white cells multiplying around the spleen, and then being released as before. With each healing the diseased area is 'seen' to be getting lighter. It is as though each healing takes the patient four steps forward. Before the next healing he takes two steps back. Then, again, at the next healing another four steps forward, then two back, each time consolidating a steady state of progress.

Viualisation in this way during healing ensures that the person's mind is engaged constructively and positively in the process of healing. As they feel the healing heat between the two hands, they are able to relate it directly to the mass of white cells which they can 'see' being formed.

During the laying on of hands and while visualisation is taking place, spoken prayers may be said giving thanks to our Lord for the healing being given.

There are those who will say, "Would it not be better if he sick person visualised Jesus Christ by their side and that He was laying His hands on them?"

This, most certainly, is a wonderful visualisation of what is, in fact, taking place. But sometimes, those new to the Christian faith need to be led gently through an experience more easily accepted, to that which is the supreme visualisation. In the last chapter, Jane was led to visualising herself walking hand in hand with Jesus, after which she confessed, 'I'm no longer the same person."

It is equally important that the mind of the one giving the ministry does not wander off onto totally irrelevant matters. One cannot, and I believe, should not, keep repeating the same prayer for healing over and over again. Ideally, one should be aware of having an open mind, given totally to God and to receiving a flow of the power of the Spirit, which is channelled into the sick person. Sometimes, however, it is not possible to achieve this state of mind and a conscious thought process is required to overcome the problem. A thought process that I adopt myself is one in which I concentrate on the name, *Jesus*. Repeating it over and over again. I 'see' each letter so large that it fills the whole of space — there is nothing else but JESUS... This is just one idea which enables me to focus my mind when it begins to wander.

When the cancer is in the lung, and the laying on of hands and visualisation have been given as just described, it helps to ask the patient to breathe in a little more deeply while hands are still laid on the chest and back. Invariably they ar able to breathe in more deeply than before the healing. I there had been pain before the laying on of hands, this wil almost certainly have been eased. This will help the breath lessness.

There are cases in which cancer may have been brough on by some shock or trauma. There are also other possibl events in life that may contribute to the onset of disease Smoking, close contact with asbestos, radiation and othe well publicised causes need no comment from me. However when people find themselves caught in an emotional trap, life-style that is foreign to them, unfulfilled ambition or relationship problem that appears impossible to resolve these are the kind of situations that, with the passage o time, can contribute to the onset of cancer. LeShan give examples in his book and in my own experience I hav found this to be borne out by those I have tried to help.

Before laying on hands, the sick person should b encouraged to talk about themselves. It is generally accepted that in many cases, sometimes referred to as 'cancer prone personalities, the onset of cancer is preceded by som traumatic event in life. This could be the death of a spouse redundancy or the experience of physical abuse. One lady told me that she watched her house burn down and she wa left with nothing more than the nightdress and dressin gown she was wearing at the time. It is such events that, for some people, within a period of two to three years, car result in cancer. It is my belief that careful counselling and psychotherapy after such encounters, could well help t avoid the onset of disease.

Cause and Effect

When Sally (not her real name), 23 years of age, had her first love affair, it resulted in a pregnancy. Her parents wanted her to have an abortion but she refused, so she was turned out of the family home and went to live in what was then known as an "unmarried mothers' home". In due course she had her baby but the social worker told her that the best thing for her and the baby was to have it adopted. Sally was desperate to keep her baby and in no way would she agree to adoption. One day, when the baby was three months old the social workers dragged the baby from her arms, insisting that it was to be adopted. The shock and trauma suffered by Sally can well be imagined. Fortunately, a lady working in the community heard of Sally's plight and fought to recover the baby for her — and, after much argument with the local authority, three months later the baby was returned to its mother.

About four years later Sally married (not the father of the baby) and the family lived what appeared to be a normal, happy life during the next fifteen years. The man Sally married was a good man who cared for his wife and child. Sadly, there seemed to be something missing in their lives. Sally felt that he was not returning her love — and she yearned to be loved. In spite of this she remained with him, desperately longing for the love and warmth which never came. Sally found herself in an emotional trap in which the relationship was incompatible. She saw no way out — and at the age of forty-two she discovered a lump in her breast — a lump, I believe, that was caused, in the first place, partly by the traumatic experience of having her baby forcibly taken away from her and later by the frustration, despair and hunger for love in the relationship with her husband.

Sally was given a lumpectomy, but within a year there was evidence of a spread of the cancer. She was admitted to hospital where she received a course of chemotherapy, but the disease seemed to have got such a hold on her, there was no improvement in her condition. We have to ask ourselves whether this was Sally's way out of the 'trap' in which she had found herself. In her unconscious mind she knew that if she got well again she would have to return to a life of stress and emotional frustration from which she longed to escape. So what was the point in getting well?

Sally's mother, father and sister, who lived in the north of England, were summoned to her bedside as it was considered that her chances of survival were slipping away fast. She discharged herself from the hospital saying that, if she was going to die, it was to be in her own home. But a friend, who had attended one of our Fellowship meetings persuaded her to be brought to Pin Mill.

Sally arrived using two walking sticks, her right eye was covered by a patch, she wore a woolly hat to keep her bald head warm and she was supported by her husband and her friend. She told me, "The cancer is in both breasts, in my head and right eye, I am partly deaf and it is also in my spine." She added, "Is that enough to be going on with?"

The last comment told me that she had not lost her sense of humour. I told her that it would do to begin with.

During the following months, her husband nursed her, cared for her every physical need and brought her to Pin Mill where Sally was given much healing prayer and laying on of hands. She was quick to learn how to use self hypnosis, to relax and enjoy visualising a return to the happy days of her childhood, running barefoot along the wide stretches of sandy beach — splashing in the clear, warm pools of water left by a receding tide.

From visualising these happy days of her childhood, I decided to take her forward to the time of her first love affair, the birth of the baby and the encounter with the social services who took the baby from her. I was pretty sure that there were mental wounds to be healed which, if left unhealed, could prevent her total healing taking place.

In hypnosis Sally was able to relive the experience of the baby being taken from her and I wanted to follow this immediately by the return of the baby which would help to ease the trauma buried deep within her unconscious mind. But I had not expected what was to come. When the baby was returned to her she cried out, "It's not the same baby. It's not my baby!" The distress in her voice told me of the agony she had suffered.

I have to confess that all I could think of doing was to try to reassure her that the baby was the same baby that was taken from her, and I then brought her out of hypnosis. When she left me she was not in the happy state that I had wished her to be.

That evening she telephoned me. Remembering everything that had happened during her visualisation of those unhappy events, she said, "Do you remember my saying that it was not the same baby?"

I said that I did.

"Well, I've been thinking about it and I'm sure I know why I reacted in that way. I had been parted from the baby for three long months, and a very young baby will grow quite a lot during that time. It was simply that she was so much bigger than when she was taken from me. That is why I said she is not the same baby." Sally had found the cause of the distress herself and asked if I could help to heal that memory.

The delightful thing about counselling with the aid of hypnosis is that the most simple and obvious suggestions can bring about a healing of the mind. She went into hypnosis and visualised holding the baby in her arms at the time just before the social workers were to come and take the baby away. I told her to tell me when they were about to remove the baby and I would tell them, in the strongest terms, to go away and leave the baby with her. When this was done, I told Sally to hold the baby tight in her arms, and to look at her and not take her gaze from her. I would then count from one to five and take her one month forward, and as I did this she would see her baby becoming a little bigger and a lot more beautiful. I repeated this by taking her forward, month by month until we were five months from the time when the baby was taken from her.

What I had done was to create within her unconscious mind a happy memory, which bridged the unhappy event and enabled her to 'see' her baby grow during the period when it had been taken from her.

Sally gradually recovered her single vision and her hearing. The hair which she had lost through the chemotherapy, grew again. She began to feel better in herself but she was left with two remaining problems. She could not walk without the sticks and when she did walk she always looked down at where she was putting her feet instead of looking ahead. It was a lack of confidence which prevented her from doing so. The other problem was that she was addicted to diamorphine (heroin), which had been given to her in hospital to control her pain level. But as she no longer had pain, she no longer had need of the drug. Without the drug, however, she suffered the well known withdrawal symptoms which demanded more drugs. It was a vicious circle.

To resolve the problem with walking, she sat in an armchair and went into a state of relaxation. I then told her to visualise standing up without the sticks, holding her head high and walking with absolute confidence. When she told me that she had done this, I told her to stand up, open her eyes and do it again.

It was a warm summer's day and the doors of our living room were open onto the garden. Sally stood up, opened her eyes and walked boldly across the room and into the garden. At the time, Doreen was looking out of one of the upstairs windows and watched as she walked slowly but firmly, stepping over some logs that had been left lying around and without noticeably looking down.

Drug Addiction

The next problem was to free Sally from the addiction to diamorphine. Whenever she refrained from taking the prescribed dose, she would suffer the withdrawal symptoms, known as 'cold turkey'. It is, I am told, a violent gnawing pain in the stomach with other side effects such as trembling and sweating. We chose an occasion when she was suffering these unpleasant symptoms and once again, Sally relaxed into a state in which she could visualise. I gave her the laying on of hands and prayed that she be released from the hold of the drug. I then placed my hand on her stomach, where she felt the pain, and told her that I was going to count from one to ten. As I counted she would receive through my hand, a spiritual 'drug' given by God, far more powerful than any man-made drug. I told her that she would feel this power entering her stomach and by the time I had counted to ten her stomach would feel filled with His power and I wanted her to tell me when she had this feeling. I kept reference to the word 'drug' as this was what her body and mind had been craving for, in this way her mind was more likely to accept the suggestion. And it did. She told me that her stomach was full of the God-given 'drug'. At this point I counted to three which 'released' the 'drug' from her stomach to flood every part of her body, creating peace where there had previously been torment. And it did just that.

It took ten days for Sally to be freed from her addiction. During that time, whenever she felt the need for diamorphine, instead of going to the bottle she telephoned me. Happily these came at regular times, so I was able to make myself available to help her.

By this time Sally was driving her car, a smart, white Ford Capri. She drove to the Lake District for a holiday and upon her return visited her parents' home to say a big "Hello" to those who had visited her in hospital.

But now we had to look at her life-style and make sure that she did not slip back into the emotional trap that had contributed to her illness.

The years of an incompatible relationship in marriage, which had almost certainly contributed to her illness, must not be allowed to continue. So Sally and her husband decided to separate.

Instead of making a clean break and giving both an opportunity for a fresh start in their lives, they decided to share the same house. It was a small, detached house. Sally occupied the first floor and her husband lived on the ground floor. They used the same front door which was equipped with two door bells — one for him and one for her. They saw each other every day. They agreed to live their own separate lives, so Sally received her friends in her part of the house and her husband entertained his friends just a few yards away, downstairs.

Sometimes, when her husband had prepared dinner for friends in his part of the house, he would take a plate of food upstairs for Sally. It was a thoughtful gesture but one which emphasised the sadness and immense frustration of the situation and added to it a feeling of rejection and isolation. While she appreciated the thought, it made her feel like an outcast and, once again, emphasised the lack of love and true companionship in her life. It was not long before she found that she was losing the use of her legs. The dis-ease within her body returned and Sally died in her room, upstairs.

We shall never know, but I venture to suggest that had Sally been counselled when the baby was taken from her, the traumatic memory of that event would have been healed before it was able to damage her health. I also suggest that had she made a clean break in her relationship with her husband after her dramatic recovery from near death, she would most likely have found the peace for which she was searching. She could have made new friends and found the love for which she was so hungry and of which she had been starved for so long, and might well have been alive today.

Chapter 11

WHY SOME AND NOT OTHERS?

No discussion on Christian healing will ever take place without someone asking why some are healed, and others are not. We shall never fully know the answer to this question. Nevertheless, we are bound to ask ourselves why one person, suffering from the same condition as another, is not healed and the other person is healed. When the same hands are used to channel Christ's healing power, it becomes even more of a mystery. Where, then, does the answer lie? There must be an answer.

Before we look more deeply into this question, let us accept that there is no greater truth than, "We are all going to die." Sooner or later, apart from tragic and fatal accidents, it will be through the malfunction of our bodies that we die. This is part of God's plan for the human race, in fact for all living creatures. There is "a time to be born and a time to die". *How* we die is what worries most people. There will be occasions when we are unaware that the end of this life is about to take place and that, through death, the new, everlasting life is about to begin. Although it is not God's will that we should suffer, it is part of His plan that we should graduate from this lowly life to the higher life within His Kingdom.

Coming back to the question, "Why some and not others?", I believe that the answer could lie partly in the relationship between the sick person and Jesus Christ. I am positive in my belief that Jesus would want that person to be whole in spirit, mind and body, just as He did those who were healed by His touch and His word during those days in Galilee.

I am convinced that all who went to Jesus in those days

asking to be healed of physical conditions, went with those conditions foremost in their minds — their blindness, leprosy, deafness, paralysis. I doubt very much whether they even considered the healing of their spirits or minds. I am equally convinced however that a large number of them grew towards wholeness in God's good time. It was the first evidence they had through physical healing, that set the process in motion... just as it does today.

There is another reason why some may not receive the healing they seek, and this concerns the relationship between the seeker and the one who lays on hands.

There is another reason why some may not receive the healing they seek, and this concerns the relationship between the seeker and the one who lays on hands.

An essential quality in the personality of the one who lays on hands is compassion and a Christian love towards the sick who come for healing, so it should not be too difficult for the 'healer' to accept the one who seeks healing. But in the strange and unusual circumstances in which the sick person finds himself, he or she is looking for someone to whom they can pour out the innermost secrets of their hearts, someone in whom they can have complete confidence. Perhaps, most important of all, it must be someone to whom they can take an instant liking. If no such rapport can be developed between the two, the sick one would be advised to go to someone else in the group.

While it is not possible to answer the question, "Why some and not others?", it is, I believe, possible to come a little closer to an answer, when questioning why someone who has received what appears to have been a complete healing does not remain healed. In other words (or in the case of Sally), why does the problem return?

God does not punish us for our sins. But it is we who punish ourselves. Guilt is the result of wrong-doing, but excessive guilt can cause sickness of the mind and sickness of the body. There is only one way for such a condition to be healed and that is through repentance and forgiveness. If wrong has been committed against an individual, that person must be asked to forgive, asking Jesus Christ also to forgive. When the prayer and the repentance are sincere, peace of mind will result. We must learn to forgive ourselves.

I have often heard people say that they thought God had given them their sickness as a punishment for their sins. No earthly father would treat even the most wayward of his children in such an unloving and callous manner, so how much less likely is our heavenly Father to inflict on us, His children, disease, suffering and pain? What I do believe is that God makes use of the sickness which, in many cases we bring upon ourselves, and, in so doing , He demonstrates His love for us through our healing. But when someone is healed in this 'supernatural' way, by the power of the Holy Spirit, they have an opportunity, even a responsibility, to be a witness to the magnificent love and power of God given to them through Jesus and, in many cases, to embrace a new way of life.

Some find it difficult to accept the idea that, after detailed examinations and the most advanced medical treatment under the care of senior consultants, something as simple as hands being placed on them in prayer, can result in any improvement in their condition. Others have decided that healing is something that only happens to other people and can never happen to them.

There are those for whom their chronic disorder has become a means of social contact, without which, neighbours would cease to ask how they are. Without realising it, they cling to the condition in which they have learned to find some comfort. For those who believe their many sins make it impossible for them to be healed, it should be explained that it was for people like them that Jesus came to live among us, and that through His death on the cross, our sins are forgiven.

Whatever may be the problem during an individual healing session it is important for the sick person to realise that Jesus hears our prayer and that there is no need (like an impatient child, pulling at its mother's apron strings) to keep on asking over and over again. It is like a gramophone needle stuck in a groove. It is sufficient to ask, to relax in faith, knowing that the prayer has been heard, and then to *surrender* and receive the healing through the laying on of hands, not forgetting to give thanks and praise.

No, I do not think we shall ever know the answer to the question, "Why are some healed and not others?" But that does not stop us wondering and examining ourselves, we who lay on hands and those of us who come to Christ asking for wholeness. We could not do better than to visualise the meetings between Jesus and those who went to Him in Galilee, to imagine the certainty and expectation in the minds of those who so went to Him, with not a doubt in their minds. They only had one problem and that was to get to Him! But since Jesus promised us that when we meet in His name, *He* will be with *us*, we do not have the problem of getting to Him. *He* is already with *us*. So let us come to Him, believing Him, trusting Him and surrendering ourselves completely to Him and *expect* to be healed, just as they did when they went to Him in Galilee.

Having said this, let us now examine some of the cases that have not been healed physically and compare them with some that have been healed.

Healing... Success or Failure?

I recall the case of Judith (not her real name), a lady of about 48 years, unmarried, with a teenage daughter.

Judith came to me asking for help with the healing of cancer of the bowel. She had a resection but there was so much spread of the tumour in the lower abdomen that no further surgery was possible. This created a complete

144

blockage in the bowel so that it soon became impossible for her to take any form of nourishment by mouth.

At the first meeting with her I found her to be a person of considerable integrity, but whose faith appeared to have taken a severe knock. It was during the laying on of hands that I felt she was not surrendering herself to being healed as I would have expected. As we talked about this she became distressed — it was almost as though a dark cloud had descended upon her — and then she told me of the great sadness in her life. She said, "I have committed the unforgivable sin, so I know that however much you or I pray for my healing, nothing will happen."

I asked Judith if she would like to tell about this 'unforgivable' sin. She explained that, some years ago, she had blasphemed against God, shouting aloud the blasphemy in her anger and despair at a certain difficult situation in her life.

"Tell me," I asked, "Are you truly sorry for what you did?"

"I would give anything to claw back those words and for them never to have been spoken."

"Then I have good news for you," I told her. "For those who truly repent of their sins, there is *always* forgiveness."

She looked at me, still with a frown but obviously wanting to know more. I asked her, "Would you like to be freed from that sin before you leave this morning?"

The response was immediate. She was sitting in the big blue chair and I sat behind her. I laid my hands on her head and simply asked Jesus to forgive her for the things she had said about God. Although it was I who started that prayer, asking for her forgiveness, it was Judith who took over from me and poured out her heart to Jesus. All the long imprisoned feelings of sorrow and despair came surging out. When she finished, tears were rolling down her face, but the frown and look of despair had gone. It was as though the tears had washed away the sadness, and, instead of the dark cloud hanging over her, she had been lifted into His light.

When she left the garden studio, she said that she felt as though she was walking on air.

Although Judith came to see me twice more at Pin Mill, when I laid hands on the tumour, there was no improvement in her physical condition. She was admitted to hospital and put on a drip.

One day during a visit to Judith in her room off the main ward, she told me of her concern for her daughter and asked if I would talk to her about Jesus. I said I would. Then she asked if I would always keep in touch with her. I said that I would do that also.

I first met her daughter during a visit to Judith in hospital. She sat by her mother's bedside with an expression of complete indifference. She spent her time fiddling with a broken drinking straw and did not speak to her mother at all.

As she left the room I followed her and stopped to speak with her in the day-room of the ward. I made it quite clear to her just how serious the situation was and that it was unlikely that her mother would live for many more days. Remembering the promise I had made to Judith, I asked the girl if she would come with me the next time I visited her mother. She agreed to do so.

We sat in my car in the hospital car park before going in, and I told the girl about the love of Jesus, and how, through prayer, He was drawing her mother closer and closer to Him for the ultimate healing, through death, into everlasting life. I told her that I wanted her to sit on one side of the bed and I would sit on the other. She was to hold one hand of her mother and I would hold the other and we would say a short prayer together. At this point the girl broke down and sobbed. She allowed her true feelings to show for the first time.

When we arrived at the bedside I told Judith that we had

146

talked of Jesus and had agreed to keep in touch always. She smiled, "I'm so glad." I then said something which, although not wholly true, was in the spirit of what was happening. I said, "She told me how very much she loves you but how difficult she has found it to tell you." With a smile full of forgiveness, she replied, "Yes, I know."

Her daughter simply sobbed her heart out. It was the best thing she could have done.

Success or failure? Judith had received forgiveness of her sin of blasphemy and her mind had been given a wonderful peace, a peace that was with her to the very end. It was a peace that so filled that tiny room that the sister and nurses remember it still. There was also the blessing of the reconciliation between Judith and her daughter who was at last able to show her love for her mother.

Judith died, but because she was able to accept the forgiving grace of Jesus, she found complete peace which filled her and supported her through to her death and to her new life with Christ.

The next case concerns a young girl who, according to medical opinion, had only a few months to live. Through living within a Christian environment and receiving the laying on of hands with relaxation, every day, she made a steady and remarkable recovery to a normal, active life. When she allowed herself to become involved in a life-style completely the opposite to that in which she had received her healing, there remained no room for the love of Christ within her. Almost immediately the disease returned. I believe we have something to learn by sharing this experience.

Neuroblastoma

Soon after we moved to Pin Mill, we were asked if we knew of anyone who had a spare bedroom and could take a seventeen-year-old girl to live with them. The girl had a form of cancer, a neuroblastoma, which strikes at children and is usually fatal. She had a twelve-month-old baby which had been taken into foster care, and, as may be guessed, she was a single parent. We had a spare bedroom and after meetings with the social workers, the girl, Angela (not her real name), was brought to the cottage.

It was suggested that she would not survive for more than two or three months. She was not brought to us with the idea of healing. It was just to give her somewhere to live during this difficult time in her life.

Doreen and I decided that if she was living with us, we would have to talk to her about Christian healing and do what we could to help her in this way also.

Angela had been a regular attender at her local church and had some awareness of the Christian faith, so I was delighted when she accepted the idea of receiving the laying on of hands. I also told her of the value of visualisation and how it could be used in her healing.

Angela was given the laying on of hands and engaged in visualisation every day. It is not often that one is able to give such sustained and regular healing, and it was encouraging to find that the cancer was not spreading. The reports from the hospital were far better than many had expected and the social workers, knowing of the healing Angela was receiving, gained new hope. They reserved judgement regarding her future and that of her baby. It was about nine months later, after much medical treatment at the Royal Marsden Hospital and continuous prayer and laying on of hands, that Angela was given a beautifully equipped ground floor apartment on a new housing estate. There was no happier girl in the whole world when we told her that she was to be given her own home in which to live with her little daughter whom she adored. With tears of joy streaming down her cheeks, she said, "I don't think my heart will stand much more!"

A Healing lost

Let us all learn from what happened next, for I believe we failed Angela.

Doreen contacted the rector of Angela's local church and told him how she had made this miraculous recovery. She asked that he did what he could to draw her into the church so that she could continue worship and build on that which she now had. Unfortunately, within a short time the rector moved to another area and contact between Angela and the church was lost.

Angela's young friends were delighted to hear that she now had her own home and it was not long before it became a meeting-place for the many young people with whom she had associated before her illness. One of these young people was the baby's father who would bring his latest girlfriend to whom he could show off his child. This naturally infuriated Angela and caused her much distress. When I visited her one Sunday morning to collect her and her baby — for she was to spend the day with us — there in the living-room was all the evidence of the previous night's activities. Drinking sessions and the showing of horrific video nasties was again a common event. Angela admitted, some time later, that she had been with some of the boys.

All this activity was in complete contrast to the life she had been living during her illness and while she was being healed by the power of God. We still kept in touch with her and sometimes she would spend the day with us in Pin Mill. It was on these occasions that we became aware of the paralysis developing in her legs.

Angela was admitted to hospital where we were able to see her more regularly and it was there that she confessed to some of the damaging practices that, I believe, had contributed to the return of the disease. One of her girlfriends visited her at her bedside in the hospital and told her that she had seen again the video in which "people were cut up and eaten". When I told the consultant of this and of the lifestyle Angela had adopted, he was horrified.

After this incident, Angela became so disturbed in her mind that only a selected few close, caring friends were allowed to see her. Angela died and her baby has been adopted by a wonderful family. Both parents are committed Christians and are active members of a Baptist Church.

I believe that Angela's mind was poisoned, her spirit violated and her body abused by the unholy happenings in her new home.

This case, more than most, emphasises the importance of the healing of the spirit and the mind if the body is to be healed and, most important, remain healed. How we could have prevented her living her life in this way, I do not know. But I do know that, when someone is given a second chance in life through the healing touch of Christ, it is essential that they receive ongoing spiritual nourishment to keep that wholeness alive within them.

Bone Cancer

Barbara (not her real name), was 30 years old, married with two small children. She had suffered from breast cancer and had a mastectomy a few years before she came to Pin Mill. Secondaries had now appeared in her skull which had been treated by chemotherapy. The treatment seemed to be successful but very severe pains had developed in the base of her spine and in her thighs.

During her first visit it became obvious that she was in far too much pain to make the journey on future occasions, so I decided to visit her in her home.

Barbara spent her days sitting on the end of a settee. Whenever she attempted to move, the tensing of her muscles caused excruciating pain, so she just remained almost motionless. Watching someone in such pain, when they are expecting you to do something about it, is one of those situations in which you are made to feel totally inadequate and realise again that the only hope lies in the power of God.

I showed Barbara how to relax and to take away the pain and, gradually, by moving very gently, she was able to lie full length on the settee. During the first visit I gave the laying on of hands, but when I left she was still in great pain.

The Power of Command

On two further occasions I visited Barbara and found her in the same terrible pain. During the laying on of hands I became angry at the state of her suffering, and remembering what Mary (who had brought me into the healing ministry) had told me about healing by the power of command, I shouted at the disease within Barbara, "In the name of Jesus Christ and by His supreme authority, I command you to leave Barbara's body. Go. Go from her now, never to return."

I think I repeated this twice. During the next visit I did the same thing. A few days later we had a telephone call from Barbara, "I've been trying to contact you but without success." Doreen took the call, and, thinking that she sounded rather excited and assuming that she was in more pain and in need of help, asked how she was.

The answer is one to be remembered, "I'm fine. I've been shopping in Ipswich!"

I am persuaded to believe that the power of the name of Jesus and His authority over the evil of disease, is as real today as it has ever been.

Barbara kept her next appointment with the consultant, not in a wheelchair as on previous occasions, but looking her most attractive best. She told me that as she walked into his consulting-room he took one look at her and, knowing that she had received Christian healing, said, "Have you been to Pin Mill?"

The story does not have a happy ending. Overjoyed at her healing, Barbara and her family went on holiday to Canada and had a wonderful time. During that holiday, Barbara experienced a pain developing in her left side and upon her return to this country, came to see me for further laying on of hands. The pain developed as the cancer spread over her body once again. She was admitted to hospital where she died.

The question I ask myself is, "Why, when Barbara received what appeared to be complete healing from the most terrible pain caused by cancer in nearly every bone in her body, did the healing not last?" Was it because she allowed the material things of life to crowd out the power of the Spirit that had taken away the disease and pain when I commanded it, in the name of Jesus, to leave her body? Was it simply a case of more secondaries developing and, this time, for reasons unknown, she was unable to receive the power of Christ's healing touch? Or perhaps it was that Jesus, hearing our prayer in the first instance, answered it with the healing for which we asked, a healing which gave Barbara that vital extra time in this life to further prepare herself for the everlasting life which was to come. The last suggestion is the one which, in the majority of similar cases, I find easiest to accept. We shall never really know nor is it for us to know. But let us never lose our faith and belief that it could have happened for Barbara a second time.

Thanks be to God for the healing she had and for her extra year of happy active life with her family.

Having said this, there are so many other joyous occasions when we find it so easy to give abundant thanks to Jesus, unconditionally, for giving us exactly that for which we asked.

Hodgkin's Disease

Take, for example the case of Lorraine. She was in her early twenties. A swelling in her neck was diagnosed as Hodgkin's disease, a cancer of the lymph glands which seems to affect young people. Sadly, her wedding had to be cancelled while she had three to four months of radiotherapy.

The treatment appeared to produce the desired results and her wedding went ahead a year later. Within three months, a lump in the groin showed that the disease had returned. This was followed by nine months of chemotherapy (up to 30 pills a day).

The steroids had caused her hands, legs and knee joints to swell and the pain was such that she was confined to a wheelchair. Next it was blood transfusions and a spell in hospital where she spent her first wedding anniversary.

Lorraine's mother worked in the same department of the hospital as Sharon, the girl who was healed of her deafness, and knowing how Sharon had been healed, she wrote to the Fellowship asking for help for her daughter. Lorraine takes up her own story:

> I shall never forget the first meeting at Pin Mill, being helped by my parents to walk from the car. I was so weak that I proceeded to fall down the small steps leading to the cottage. Eventually I was guided to the summerhouse in the garden.
>
> After the first laying on of hands and experiencing the calmness and the heat surging through me, my health improved quite remarkably. After many more sessions and an increasing awareness of the sense of wholeness and revitalisation, I have reached the stage at which I am today.
>
> Many people have remarked how well I look and, believe me, it's not half as good as I feel.
>
> Before all this began, my husband and I had faith, and despite the many difficulties faced over the past two years, neither of us has lost that faith. In fact, through the many prayers of the people from our own church

and the prayers and healing of the Pin Mill Fellowship, our faith has been considerably strengthened.

I don't think, I *know* that our Lord's healing hand has been at work.

For anyone who might still be sceptical about this, just remember, everything is possible through prayer. The Pin Mill Fellowship is, to me, an extension of that prayer by providing physical and spiritual healing, although for some the healing process may be slower and less dramatic than others."

Lorraine and her devoted husband attend our Fellowship meetings regularly. Although not members of our church, they also come and join with us in worship whenever we have a healing service.

Today, Lorraine is a fit, healthy, attractive young woman enjoying a full and active life. It is another good reason for saying, "Praise the Lord!"

Guilt can kill

In sharp contrast, when guilt weighs so heavily that the sick person cannot forgive themself and cannot accept forgiveness from Jesus Christ, their last days are spent in torment.

A certain lady came to see me. She had become the lover of a married man whose wife had cancer. One day, during an argument between the two women, the wife said, "I hope that one day you suffer as I am suffering."

The lady was not sure whether she, the wife, was referring to suffering through cancer or suffering through the loss of her husband to another woman. A short while later the wife died.

The question grew in the mind of the lady who could never separate the two, and it was not long before the thought became a reality. She developed cancer in exactly the same place as the wife's tumour. She was convinced that she had done wrong in coming between man and wife and confessed to strong feelings of guilt. Nothing that was done through prayer and laying on of hands could change this strong feeling of guilt. She could not forgive herself for coming between man and wife, and she could not ask for the forgiveness of the wife she believed she had wronged, because she was dead. As a result, she could get nowhere near to accepting forgiveness from Christ. Her last days were spent in a state of distress and she died as she knew she would.

Bitterness can kill

Very few healings occur without further knowledge being gained. We are learning all the time and are privileged to be given crumbs of knowledge from the table of our Lord. Let me tell you of one of the crumbs which I picked up some years ago and which has been foremost in my mind when ministering to people during their first laying on of hands.

I started this book with the story of the healing of Ken, a man who had cancer in his right arm. It had been there for ten, long, agonising years and, having had all the treatment that caring medical science could offer him, the tumour was still there and he was about to have his arm amputated.

In my prayer for his healing, I had asked that all thoughts of bitterness, resentment and anger be washed from his mind as these were blocks to the work of the Holy Spirit within us. As I have recalled in the first chapter, during the laying on of hands, Ken saw a vision of Jesus Christ standing beside his chair and was healed instantly of the cancer and the pain which had plagued him for the previous ten years.

About four months later we held a meeting in the cottage for those members of the Fellowship who had started to lay on hands. Ken had joined us as he wanted to find some way in which he could contribute to our ministry. I had been talking about the importance of the healing of the spirit and how the healing of the body is likely to be determined by the state of the spirit and mind, when Ken said that he had something to tell us.

Ken, you may remember, was a milkman. He had an extensive country area to serve, including a large military air base, and was well known and liked by many hundreds of people whom he met almost daily on his round. Back at the dairy, however, all was not well.

Ken's friend had been employed at the dairy depot and had been made redundant. This was accepted philosophically, though rather sadly, for his friend enjoyed the work. Within a couple of weeks of his friend leaving, another man, much younger, was appointed to do the same job. This made Ken very angry, and recognising what he believed to be the injustice of the situation, went to the management in an effort to get his friend reinstated. His efforts were useless, so he went to the union to see if they could help.

"I was so angry, I was really stirring up trouble for the dairy and the newly appointed man." he told us. "I have to admit that I had begun to hate this new man although it was no fault of his that my friend had been put out of a job. All the time that I was involved in this campaign against the dairy and the man, the pain began to come back in my arm."

Ken continued, "Two weeks ago, on a Friday evening after a long day on my round, I was sitting in the kitchen and the pain in my arm was almost as bad as it had even been. Then my mind went back to the time when I was given my healing and I remembered what had been said in prayer, about getting rid of all bitterness and resentment and anger before my healing could take place. Then I thought — all the time I've been causing trouble I've been creating the very bitterness and resentment of which I was told to be rid, so I went to the bottom of the garden, shut myself in the tool-shed, got down on my knees and said, "Please God forgive me for what I've been doing." Do you know, before

I had got up off my knees the pain had left me, and it has never come back."

Ken is a witness to the healing power of God through Jesus Christ. When I last spoke with him, he told me that hardly a day goes by when he has not been asked by one of the many people he meets during his daily round, to tell the story of the day Jesus came to him and healed him of cancer. And he still enjoys telling them. Every day he is a witness for Christ.

That healing and the incident that followed was nine years ago. I still see Ken two or three times a year. On the anniversary of his healing we give thanks for it and for his arm which is good and strong. Praise the Lord!

No further comment from me is needed to emphasise the importance of the healing of the spirit and the cleansing of the mind when giving the laying on of hands for physical healing — *and* just as important, in keeping that healing. I have said it several times already. But it is important.

Troubled Mind — Sick Body

During the first discussion I have with a patient, I try to discover what their true expectations are, and whether their spirits are high or low.

One young lady, Helen (not her real name), discovered a lump in her breast and went to her GP. He examined her and assured her that there was nothing to worry about. Six months later, she went to another doctor, because the lump was still there and a little bigger. He lost no time in arranging a biopsy which confirmed that the lump was malignant. The breast tumour was dealt with by lumpectomy. Further examination revealed that, because of the delay in dealing with the original tumour, the cancer had spread to her liver and, understandably, Helen was angry that the first doctor had given her such wrong advice. She was then told that she should have a course of chemotherapy to deal with the second tumour. It was at this stage in her illness that Helen came to Pin Mill asking for help. At our first meeting she said, "I don't think I could ever cope with being well again."

Helen was disillusioned, depressed, very bitter and in no state to receive physical benefit from Christian healing. First, I had to get her to see that life was worth living and that there was real hope in the promises made by Jesus. Fortunately she had a sound Christian faith upon which we were able to build.

Helen began to talk about her childhood and her school days. They seemed to be a mixture of happy events tinged with an underlying sadness. As she recalled the events of her early teenage years, she began to both laugh and cry. The very real unhappiness in her life at that time — she was thirteen — was that she felt she was not developing, physically, as the other girls were. She was tall, thin and flat-chested. At the age of fourteen the other girls began to develop breasts and some were even wearing their first bra. Helen, on the other hand, showed no real signs of such envied development. The mixture of laughter and tears was explained when Helen told me that the girls laughed at her thin, undeveloped figure and, sad and distressed though she was, she felt the best thing was to laugh with them.

It was not until she was sixteen that her mother bought Helen her first bra.

Unfortunately, that was not the end of the trauma. Within a few years, Helen, an attractive young woman, was being dated by young men friends. She told me that the unhappiness resulting from her slow physical development, and having been the subject of ridicule at school, had never left her. Was she going to disappoint them by what she regarded as her lack of sexuality?

From the age of thirteen to twenty-six, Helen's main worry in life was therefore about the shape and size of her breasts. The mental strain and anxiety concerning her relationship with men together with her obsession regarding her physical development, was all focussed on her breasts. Where did the cancer start?

The problem had not been helped by the scar and slight hollow in her left breast resulting from the lumpectomy.

I talked to Helen about meditation and visualisation using the powerful imagery of her unconscious mind. She told me of the things she enjoyed doing before she became ill. What stood out was her love of swimming. I asked her if she would like to go to an island in the South Pacific where there were hot white sands, palm trees on the shore, clear blue seas, a warm sun with a cool fresh breeze. There was a hint of a smile on Helen's face as she said, "Oh, that really would be lovely."

Helen learned to use her mind and to visualise. In this way she was able to find herself on the island. It was as real to her as the most vivid dream. She went for a swim and discovered that she could swim under water without having to hold her breath! She told me of all the wonderful marine life. She found a friendly dolphin that allowed her to ride on its back. When we finished the session she talked about the experience and laughed about the very idea of riding on a dolphin. Her mind had been stimulated by a happy event that she could draw upon in quieter moments. She was able to realise that all was not lost, life was worth living and new hope was given to her.

Helen was ready to ask for and receive the healing power of Christ.

The first thing the consultant remarked upon when he next saw her was the great improvement in her spirits. In fact Helen told me that her friends also remarked on her change of attitude. She came to know that island in the sun with all its charms, and she became more hopeful, open and expectant. This was a far better state in which to receive the healing power of the Spirit.

Regular sessions of visualisation, prayer and laying on of

hands together with the chemotherapy, resulted in a slight reduction of the swelling of the liver. Her own GP was the first to note this.

A member of Helen's own church commented on how much better she was looking and asked how she accounted for this. When she explained that she was having Christian healing by the laying on of hands together with visualisation, Helen was told that she should not be receiving healing in this way and that any healing she needed could be given by those who would pray for her in her own church. She was persuaded not to return to me for further healing. Within three to four weeks Helen was admitted to hospital and a few weeks later she died.

We shall never know whether Helen would have made a complete recovery if she had continued to receive healing in the way we had both agreed. What we do know is that to all observers, Helen was making progress. Most important of all, Helen, herself, was convinced that she was being healed. I mention this case because it demonstrates, once again, the influence of the mind over the body and its important role in healing. It also shows the damage that can be caused by ill-informed attitudes and comment.

A new Spark of Life

I received a telephone call from a man asking if I would go to the hospital to see his wife, Eileen (not her real name). He explained that she had cancer and that the consultant had told him there was nothing more he could do to help her and that she had probably no more than twelve to fourteen days to live. He suggested that he phoned me as Christian healing was the only chance his wife had left.

When I arrived at the hospital Eileen was in a side ward by herself. She was in her late sixties and looked very frail. As I spoke to her she was vomiting and obviously not in a state to receive visitors — particularly a stranger who wanted to talk to her about Christian healing. She had been told why I was coming to see her so all I did was to ask if she would like me to lay my hand on her head and say a prayer. As I was doing this she became more relaxed and gave the appearance of wanting to go to sleep. I took this as my cue to leave, saying that I would come back another day.

The following day Eileen's husband telephoned me saying that her condition had improved a little and would I go to see her again as soon as possible, so I gave a second and longer laying on of hands and was able to talk with Eileen as she was obviously far more comfortable than when I first saw her.

Again I received a call to announce further improvement in her condition and a further request for more visits.

Arrangements had been made some time previously for Eileen to go to the new hospice in Colchester and within a day or two she was moved. Unfortunately, Colchester is a little too far for me to make regular calls so I asked a member of our Fellowship who lives not far from Colchester to visit her and report back to me. The report was something like this... "I've been to see Eileen. Did you know that she is up and about?" I said that I did not. "She is walking about the ward and has developed such an appetite that the cooks wanted to know who the lady was who eats everything they put on the plate." My friend then added, "The Sister has told her that the hospice is not for people like Eileen. It is for sick people. She should go home and look after her family."

Eileen returned home to look after her husband and her son and came to see me once more. We talked about continuing with the laying on of hands about once a month, but no matter how much she was persuaded by her family to continue with the healing, in no way would she agree to come. She simply said that she was fine now — and "thank you very much", but she needed no more help.

About a year later I met her in the hospital car park. She

was having difficulty in walking and told me that the cancer had returned. She died a few weeks later.

When I spoke to the consultant about her healing, he said, "She was dying. Whatever you did, she was given a new spark of life and recovered."

Could it be that the new spark of life was starved of spiritual nourishment, and became extinguished?

Brain Tumour

The question, "Why are some healed and some not healed?", becomes even more difficult to answer when I think of Sylvia. She was in her early fifties, a beautiful person physically and spiritually, a very loving and much-loved lady. Sylvia had had a mastectomy some years before we met. She came to me when the disease returned and she was diagnosed as having a tumour in the brain. It was devastating news for her friends and family.

If ever I was asked to describe a personality most likely to receive the benefits of Christian healing, I would have described Sylvia. She was a lady with great faith, indeed an almost childlike faith. Nothing was complicated. Simple and trusting, she lived her life close to her Lord.

It cannot be denied that many prayers for the relief of Sylvia's suffering were answered. When she first began to lose the use of her legs, the strength returned to them after the laying on of hands and she was able to go on holiday. But it was not long before the problem returned. Soon she was unable to walk without a frame, and within a short while she became confined to her bed where, a few days later, this very dear lady received the final healing through death.

So just as we think we are beginning to understand the way God works, something happens that makes us realise that knowing such things is simply not for us — yet. Our job is to have and keep faith in Jesus, to trust Him and to know that, in a way we shall never understand, God's almighty plan is being worked out.

God working through Sickness

The cancer that had developed within John de St Croix, the minister I collected from hospital and took to Mary for healing, (chapter 1) was a tragedy. At the time it seemed a great injustice. Here was a man who was devoting his life to God. He was married with three teenage boys and in the prime of life with so much to give to the Christian Church. I am quite sure that God saw this as much of a tragedy as we did, but He did something about it.

John responded to our prayers and to the laying on of hands. To the amazement of the consultants, he began his return to work. Shortly after this, due to an unfortunate incident in his further treatment, John died.

But just see how God had used John's illness! During his initial healing, when we saw the improvement in his condition, I was convinced that the power of God was a living power and ours for the asking. Without our taking one decision, we have moved to Pin Mill and witnessed the development of what must be one of the busiest fellowships in the country, with the sick now coming to us from all parts of the UK, and our work with doctors and hospitals growing stronger all the time.

All this has been brought about by the power of the Holy Spirit, initially through the sickness, the healing and the eventual death into glory, of John de St Croix.

PRAISE THE LORD!

Chapter 12

MORE CASE STUDIES

It is by the sharing of healing experiences that we are able to help those who come asking for Christ's ministry. In the belief that we learn something from every healing I offer the following detailed case studies.

School Phobia or Possession?

Rachel (not her real name), a girl of eleven years of age, had been ill most of her life. Her mother brought her to me and in telling me of her daughter's medical history, said that Rachel had a dread of school and had never been able to complete a school term. As soon as the term commenced she would develop an illness. Her current condition was one which her frustrated GP, hospital consultant, psychologist and hypnotherapist had been unable to resolve.

Rachel simply could not expand her chest to breathe. Her chest muscles were 'locked' so that she was unable to inhale in the normal manner. She flexed her diaphragm with little jerks and in this way was able to take in air but, of course, in very small amounts.

There were certain exceptions to this way of breathing. When she was asleep at night she breathed quite normally, then, as soon as she awoke she coughed and in the act of coughing she was able to inhale and exhale, but, as soon as she stopped coughing, her chest locked. Stranger still, she would cough at certain times during the day, and precisely at those times she would inhale and exhale. Then when the coughing finished, the chest locked once again. Her mother wrote down the times during the day when she would

164

cough. There was nothing vague about these times. The coughs would come at specific times such as 10.23 am and the next would be at 1.41 pm — about six times during the day. The remarkable thing was that the coughing phenomenon would occur exactly on time when Rachel had no access to a watch or clock.

The condition frightened the child and something had to be done to 'unlock' her chest, even for short periods.

Rachel was a highly intelligent child so I explained to her that the power of Jesus could 'unlock' her chest and she would be able to breathe normally. It was vitally important that she believed me, so, to ensure that there would be no doubt in her mind, and remembering that Rachel had already been introduced to hypnosis by the medical authority, I asked her if she would like to concentrate on her healing while in hypnosis, to which she readily agreed.

She went into hypnosis and I laid my hands on her head and prayed aloud to Jesus asking him to unlock Rachel's chest so that she could breathe normally. By praying in a conversational manner, she was able to identify more closely with Jesus and know that she would be able to breathe again. I placed my right hand on her chest and told her that, in a moment, she would be able to breathe normally. After two or three minutes I told her to start breathing in, gently at first, then becoming deeper and deeper. This she did. The child was relieved and her mother delighted.

A telephone call that evening told me that the breathing had lasted until 7.30 pm when Rachel started coughing, at the end of which her chest locked as before. I asked to see her the following day and within sixty seconds of placing my hand on her chest, she could breathe normally.

Whether this condition was induced to protect her from school or not, it was quite clear that her inability to breathe caused her great distress. I asked her if she would like me to give her control over this situation and to be able to 'unlock' her chest herself whenever she wanted to. She appeared to welcome the idea. I first relaxed her in hypnosis, then placed one hand on her head and with the other I took her right hand, placed it on her chest and asked Jesus to give Rachel the power to 'unlock' her chest whenever she needed to. In this way she was given the ability to relieve herself of the panic and distress whenever her chest locked. It also gave relief to her parents who, by this time, were becoming quite desperate. In spite of the girl being given relief in this way, her mother told me that when she left me, having been given the ability to breathe properly, she cried. It was only when she began coughing and her chest locked again, that she became her normal self — not exactly happy but certainly less miserable than when she could breathe normally!

It became more and more obvious that this was a condition induced to protect her from going to school. The social services had suggested that Rachel went to boarding school and had threatened her parents with a court case if their wishes were not carried out, so the pressure was on the whole family.

In conversation with her parents I learned that Rachel had claimed that a little girl named Julie was living inside her and that Julie told her to do and say the bad things that she did. For example, Doreen gave her a small wooden cross to wear around her neck. When she got home she threw it across the room, explaining later that it was Julie who did it, not Rachel.

Although it would have been easy to dismiss this as childish fantasy, I decided to believe her and deal with it through prayer and the laying on of hands. When Rachel told me about Julie, I suggested to her that Julie was probably a little girl who lived a long time ago and had died having had a very bad cough. I went on to suggest that when she died there was no one who really loved her who prayed to Jesus asking Him to look after her and take her into the new life that was waiting for her. I then asked Rachel if she would like me to ask Jesus to take Julie away from her and to live with Him and be given new friends in her new life. She agreed that we should do this.

By now Rachel was quite happy receiving her healing while in hypnosis so I suggested that she should do the same on this occasion, then she would be quite sure that Julie had left her. I sat behind her and laid my hands on her head and prayed aloud to Jesus, "please Jesus, will you take Julie away from Rachel. Take her with you into her new life so that she may make new friends and be happy for ever and ever. Amen."

I remained silent, and after a few moments Rachel said, "She's gone."

When we finished the healing, I said that I was sure she was quite right, but why was she so certain that Julie had gone? She replied, "Because I saw her go."

On the journey home she said, "Mummy, you've no idea how good it is to see through just one pair of eyes once again."

I offer no explanation — just praise the Lord for answering our prayer. Julie never returned... and Rachel went to school.

Myalgic Encephalomyelitis

Simon was a healthy, happy and very active 13-year-old boy who loved his school and all the school activities. He came from a happy, stable and loving family background.

He awoke one morning with a gastric viral infection which led to six months of intensive worry for his parents. He developed diarrhoea, severe headaches, dizziness and vomiting. His doctor prescribed Stugeron which seemed to clear things up and he returned to boarding-school.

Within a few days he awoke feeling dizzy and was sent home once again. He was put back on Stugeron, but after three weeks his condition worsened and he was admitted to hospital for investigations, lumbar puncture, blood tests and X-rays.

After six days Simon was sent home with no real diagnosis and was re-admitted ten days later for a brain scan, EEG and neurological surgeon's comments. He diagnosed a psychiatric disorder but the paediatrician was not convinced that this was so, and Simon was given more tests followed by ENT and balance tests.

When the psychiatric disorder was diagnosed, it was arranged for Simon to visit Great Ormond Street Hospital where the diagnosis was confirmed. By this time Simon could not walk unless he had support on both sides. To get around his home by himself he had to crawl on his hands and knees.

A child psychiatrist visited him at his home and prescribed intensive physiotherapy. Over a period of weeks, there was a slow but only slight improvement. The psychiatrist said that the condition was a 'one-off' disturbance caused by deep-seated fear.

After a week-end of severe depression, Simon's mother telephoned me asking if I would see him. They arrived by car and I asked that I should have a talk with Simon's mother before seeing him. He could sit in the car until we were ready. After I had been given the background to his case, I asked Doreen if she would bring Simon into the cottage. We had no idea just what a problem this would present. He had absolutely no balance whatsoever, but somehow they covered the few yards from car to cottage without Simon collapsing into a heap on the ground. He could only stand by himself by holding on to something firm and solid.

Having explained my intention to his mother and gained her agreement for the way in which I was going to give the laying on of hands, I was then able to explain to Simon how he was going to be healed of this extreme dizziness.

Simon had been through six months of tests, hospitals and yet more tests without any real improvement in his condition. It would not therefore have surprised me if he had little faith in his problems being resolved merely by someone placing their hands on his head. It was vitally important that he did not doubt that he was about to be healed and that he was able to concentrate wholly on what I was saying and doing. I could help him in both ways by relaxing him in hypnosis.

Simon, like most young people, was a very good subject. He sat in a comfortable armchair and when he was relaxed in this way, I sat behind him and placed my hands on his head. His mother sat nearby and could witness all that I was about to do. First I prayed aloud for the healing of his spirit, mind and body and asked Jesus to take away all the dizziness from Simon's head. I felt it important that Simon participated in his healing as much as possible. I wanted him to visualise his healing taking place and to tell me what was happening.

I told him that, having prayed to be given the power to heal him, the power of God, given to us through Jesus, would draw out of his head all the dizziness. I found myself calling this power the 'God-power'. It was a word which I had never used before in healing, certainly a word that had never entered my mind until that moment!

I told Simon that the God-power was 'sucking' the dizziness out of his head and into my hands. When he felt it going, I wanted him to tell me. After some five minutes he said he could feel the dizziness being 'sucked' out of him, so I asked him where he wanted me to move my hands. In this way he directed his own healing by telling me where to place my hands. After half an hour of placing my hands on the places to which he had directed me, he announced that all the dizziness had gone. I told him to be sure that it had all gone. He said he was sure, so I asked him to open his eyes while still remaining in hypnosis. He looked around the room without experiencing any dizziness whatsoever. I then told him to shut his eyes again and stand up holding my hands. I stood in front of him, facing him while he merely touched the tips of my fingers to give a sense of direction. As I walked backwards around the room, Simon followed me without the slightest sign of unsteadiness then back to the armchair where he sat down and I brought him out of hypnosis. I asked him if he would like to stand up and walk about as he was healed of the dizziness. He stood up and walked about. *There was no dizziness.* In fact, to show just how steady he was he gave an impression of a stork and stood on one leg.

Experience has taught me that certain conditions which are healed almost instantly sometimes require a follow-up healing, particularly after a long and distressing illness. I arranged therefore to see Simon on two more occasions, leaving one day between each of the sessions. Two days later he arrived with his mother, asleep in the back of the car. They had just returned from the hospital where he had been for his physiotherapy. One can only assume that the physiotherapist, seeing her patient make such a sudden recovery, increased the exercises which she was convinced had been the cause of the change in his condition and Simon was so exhausted he had fallen asleep. There was no point in my seeing him as I wanted him to be as alert as possible. His mother said she would bring him back later in the day, but Simon needed the remainder of that day to recover. He slept all day.

Unfortunately, I could not see him for another ten days during which time he had slipped back into his condition and the dizziness returned.

It was clear to us that we had the answer to his problem, so we simply started again, making sure that he would be able to see me on three occasions with one day between each session. This we did and he was completely healed. After six months of tests and treatment to decide upon a diagnosis, without improvement in his condition, through prayer, faith and the laying on of hands, Simon was healed.

Food Allergy

Debbie, a young woman of 24 years, was a professionally trained nanny. She came to Pin Mill as nanny to the twin babies of friends of ours and it was while preparing lunch that Doreen was told that Debbie could not eat this and she could not eat that. There was not much that she could eat.

Debbie tells her own story:

> While living in Dallas, Texas, I began to notice I was needing more and more sleep. During Easter 1984 I quite happily slept for three days. Returning to England in 1985 I visited a doctor who diagnosed food allergies due to a large overdose of cortisone.
>
> Through tests and exclusion diet, we discovered that I was allergic to beef, lamb, pork, wheat, dairy products, tea, coffee, chocolate, sugar, yeast, coconut and alcohol.
>
> By cutting out the offending foods my life began to improve and I had a lot more energy, however, sometimes I would give in to a 'bad' food or perhaps someone would prepare a vegetarian meal for me and use cheese and I would be loth to hurt their feelings. Also, restaurants were not always precise when they told me the ingredients of their dishes.
>
> The result of these mistakes varied. Often I would immediately fall asleep (wherever I happened to be). Sometimes my face would swell, usually around the eyes or the neck, like mumps. There would also be sickness or fainting. After a binge at a party when I had indulged in Pavlova, cheese, bread and punch, I slept for a long time and within days had an awful rash on my face. But, for me, by far the worst reaction was depression and a tendency to be thoroughly nasty to people which afterwards I really regretted and for which I hated myself.
>
> Last November I made a social visit to Pin Mill with some friends and after explaining that there were a couple of things I couldn't eat at lunch, Jeff gave me

healing by the laying on of hands and visualisation. The result was immediate and now I am able to lead a normal life again. Thank you, God, for enabling people to give us your great gift of healing.

Debbie describes her symptoms well and we get a good idea of just how much this must have affected her life. But let me explain just how simple it is to heal such a condition.

Before lunch, I took Debbie into the studio and first explained fully what we were about to do. She lay on the couch and I showed her how to relax in hypnosis so that she would be able to visualise her healing taking place.

First, I laid hands on her head and we said a prayer for her healing. Next she was told to visualise being in her home with some of the foods to which she was most allergic on the table before her. I then told her that I wanted her to eat some of these foods. She selected cheese as representing dairy produce and a slice of wholemeal bread spread with butter. It was something she longed to be able to eat. We reminded ourselves that all good, wholesome food is given to us by God that it might nourish our bodies, not harm them. I then asked her to eat the bread and cheese which she had visualised. As she did so I would place my hand on her throat. As she began to eat I moved my hand down her body over the whole of her digestive system — stomach and abdomen — healing her as my hand moved over her. I did this three times with each of the foods she could 'see' before her in her unconscious mind.

I then asked her how long it would be, in normal circumstances, before the allergy developed. Whether it was hours or days I took her ahead to the appropriate time and told her to tell me how she felt. On each occasion she declared that all was well. I took her forward a further few days and again she told me that all was well, whereupon I reassured her that she was healed and that in future she would be able to eat these foods without any ill effect.

Finally, I brought her out of hypnosis and asked her, now that she was healed, what she would most like to eat. The answer came without delay, "A big cheese sandwich!"

We went into the cottage and enjoyed a lunch which, for Debbie, included a large cheese sandwich. There was no allergic reaction.

Debbie's job takes her to different parts of the world and from time to time we hear from her. A recent telephone call informed us that she is now an air stewardess. Always the news is good. Her life has been changed and she can eat whatever she likes.

Since Debbie's healing I have used the same approach in the healing of others who have been living on the most severely restricted diets, and I am happy to say that all have been healed.

Animal and Dust Allergy

Debbie's is not an isolated case. I have dealt with a number of similar allergies in the same way. There was an example, Susanne, 39 years, a hairdresser who suffered from a blocked nasal passage which was aggravated by the chemical sprays used in her job. It seemed that she was always sneezing.

A medical examination showed that the nasal membranes were "3 to 4 times the size they should be". She was told that dairy produce caused the trouble and adjusted her diet accordingly. After a few weeks there was a marked improvement and she could breathe through her nose. But she still sneezed when she came in contact with dust, making the bed, being near cats, dogs and horses.

After about two years, although she kept to the strict diet, the nasal membranes became swollen once again.

In hypnosis I was able to lay hands on her head and nose while she visualised stroking a dog with no ill effect.

Susanne explains:

This was all done with healing prayer. In my mind I

saw a friendly little dog and I got really close to it and stroked it. I was told that in future I would never have any more trouble when I was with dogs, cats and horses, etc. I was shown how I could overcome any worries. Then, just to prove to me that I was healed, a small spaniel was brought to me and I got very close to it. I stroked it and fed it some biscuits, all this with no ill-effect whatsoever. Usually I would be sneezing but here I was stroking a dog and no trouble. I felt great, so relaxed. This healing has helped me with my confidence and, since that afternoon in April, my allergy has gone. So all I can say is, "Thank you, Lord." I cannot say that I understand what has happened, but thank you.

Post-Operative Immobility

Brenda, a lady in her 50's, had suffered from severe arthritis in her hips and it was decided to give her a hip replacement, first on the left side, and when this had healed, to replace the right hip.

For the first operation she was given a general anaesthetic and the surgery was completely satisfactory.

It could be seen from the X-rays of her right hip-joint that the bone forming the socket was literally crumbling away. The pain was almost constant and the only relief she had was through the laying on of hands. This gave her freedom from pain for two or three days and enabled her to sleep at night.

Within a few months Brenda was given her second hip replacement, but on this occasion it was decided to give her an epidural injection instead of a general anaesthetic.

She was first given an intravenous injection to render her unconscious while still in her room, so did not remember leaving her bed. The next thing she remembered was waking up, back in her room, and the operation was over.

Within a few days she was encouraged to get out of bed

and exercise the new hip, but try as she might she could not move that right leg. She was given crutches to help her walk, but the right leg had no power.

For nearly three months Brenda walked on crutches. The surgeon arranged for her hip to be X-rayed and the plates had shown that the operation had been totally successful, but still she could not use that leg. She just dragged it along between the crutches.

About this time I heard a programme on BBC Radio 4, when doctors were talking about the problem of patients who could not move their limbs after undergoing successful surgery. They discussed a theory that this condition occurred after patients had been given an epidural injection when, although the conscious mind had been anaesthetised by an intravenous injection, the unconscious mind was still able to register everything that was taking place during surgery. The programme presenters asked any listeners who might have such problems, to contact the BBC and arrangements would be made for them to see a hypnotherapist, at no cost to the listener.

Without telling Brenda of these details, I asked her if she would like me to take away the paralysis in her right leg. This was the only occasion when I have *not* discussed with the subject the details of what was to follow. I merely asked her if she would trust me to do the right thing for her.

Brenda lay on the couch and before going into hypnosis I laid hands on her and prayed for the recovery of the use of her right leg. I then asked her if she could lift her left leg off the couch. She showed me that she could. I then asked if she could lift her right leg off the couch. There was no way, try as she may, that she could move that leg. It was as though it was paralysed.

Brenda went into hypnosis and I asked her to visualise arriving at the reception of the hospital where she had the surgery. I then took her through being admitted and having the first intravenous injection, a period which she could recall in her conscious mind. Next, I told her that I wanted her to tell me everything that happened from the moment she was wheeled away on the trolley to the moment when she was returned to her room, the memory of which was not in her conscious mind. This she did in a surprising amount of detail. During her recall of events I commented favourably and positively on the way in which the operation was proceeding. At each point when she became distressed, I suggested that the surgeon and all those assisting him were doing a splendid job and when they had finished, she would be able to walk, even run, once again.

This session was recorded on audio tape so that it could be examined afterwards. Brenda spoke of the manner in which the epidural was given. She was given four intravenous injections in her left wrist during the course of the operation. She spoke of the noise of sawing and banging and said that, while she could not feel pain in her right hip, she had a sensation of pushing and pressure on the leg. She repeated comments made by the surgeon and anaesthetist, such as, "I shall need her here a little longer to clean her up." And a comment was made that the bone of her hip socket was crumbling away which had made the operation more difficult. She spoke of 'sutures', of the metal shaft that was to be cemented into the femur, and other terms of which she had no previous knowledge. Finally there was comment that she was not 'coming round' as expected after the surgery was over so something was given to her in the recovery room. At this point I brought her out of hypnosis but, before doing so, I told her that she would remember nothing of what had happened except that the operation had been a wonderful success and her leg was now healed and she could move it. I felt there was nothing to be gained by allowing this rather traumatic experience to dwell in her conscious mind when it had not been there in the first place.

Brenda opened her eyes and asked, "How did I do? Was I alright?"

176

"What do you remember?" I asked.

The reply was what I had hoped for, "I don't remember anything, except that my leg is alright."

She was still lying on the couch. "Now you can lift your right leg off the couch."

She first bent her knee, then, with little effort, lifted the right leg about eighteen inches off the couch. Brenda was healed and we gave thanks to our Lord.

She phoned me the next day to tell me that she no longer needed the crutches and had been for a half-mile walk.

It is worth asking what had happened that prevented Brenda from walking after what had been successful surgery. My explanation is that, although her conscious mind was rendered 'inactive' by means of the intravenous injection, her unconscious mind was far from inactive. Her ears were doing their job of registering sound, and these sounds were being communicated to the unconscious mind. The problem, I believe, had been caused by those in the operating theatre not being aware that this was taking place. The unguarded comments of the surgeon and anaesthetist, together with the disturbing noises of sawing and hammering, had caused such trauma in her unconscious mind, that she was left with the depressing thought that the operation had not been a success.

The power of her unconscious mind over her body was enough to convince her that she could not move the leg, and, indeed, she could not move it for nearly three months after the operation.

I wonder what would have happened if Brenda's ears had been plugged so that she could have heard nothing of the events during surgery. Or, if it had been possible, to connect her to a personal tape recording of her favourite music?

A short while after this healing, I was able to play the tape to a friend who had assisted at Brenda's operation. It was confirmed that the events recalled by Brenda and recorded on the tape were, in fact, as my friend had remembered them during the surgery.

A year later, Brenda asked me if she could hear the tape. She felt that long enough had passed for the events not to worry her. She found it most interesting to hear herself talking about an occasion in her life of which she had no conscious memory. A short while later she told me that she was quite sure that, had we not been able to discover and heal the traumatic memory lying in her unconscious mind, she would still be unable to have the use of that leg.

Brain Tumour — Inability to swallow

John was 24-years-old. He had a brain tumour. It was in the centre of his brain and was inoperable. He had had two courses of radiotherapy, which meant that he had lost all his hair. But the big problem was that he could not swallow. I was told by one of the doctors that the tumour was affecting the part of his brain that controls his ability to swallow, and that there was nothing that I could do to overcome the problem.

John had come to me for the laying on of hands which, of course, he was given with prayers for the healing of the tumour. But unless we could get some nourishment into him he would be unable to gain enough strength to fight the disease and to make the journey to Pin Mill to receive the laying on of hands and further healing.

I decided that this was a case for John's own mind to overcome the problem of swallowing and felt quite sure that this could be helped by hypnosis. I discussed the problem with him and explained, in detail, what I was proposing to do. John welcomed the idea.

"What is your favourite food, John?" I asked.

The answer was short and direct, "Cheese."

"How would you like to eat a freshly grilled, sizzling welsh rarebit — and with it a glass of chilled milk?"

178

John smiled and said that he would like that very much indeed. So I showed him how he could use his own mind to visualise the welsh rarebit and the milk in front of him. When he told me that he could 'see' the food I told him that if he licked his lips he would be able to 'taste' the cheese — and that he would also 'smell' it. It is important to make quite clear that the 'seeing' and 'smelling' of the food was as real to John as though he did actually have it before him. He was using that part of his mind that is used when dreaming — we all know how very real dreams can be.

As he sat there, licking his lips, I laid my hands on his head and asked Jesus to heal John in spirit, mind and body. I placed my hand on his throat and asked that he be healed of his problem of swallowing. This done, I told John that there was a knife and fork on the table before him and he would be able to eat the tasty dish without any problem.

As he was having this very real 'dream' of eating his favourite food, I watched his mouth and throat move as though he was actually eating and swallowing the food. I told him to tell me when he had finished eating and drinking. While this was going on, Doreen was in the kitchen preparing a real welsh rarebit. It was cut into small squares and with it was a glass of cold milk.

John told me that he had finished eating and there had been no problem with either the cheese or the milk. Next came the important step of eating and drinking the real food.

I asked John, "Would you now like to have another welsh rarebit and another glass of milk?" I added, "You will find no difficulty in eating it and you will enjoy it just as much as you did the first one."

John did not hesitate. He accepted my suggestion. At this point Doreen placed before him the real food and drink. I did not bring John out of hypnosis but simply suggested that if he opened his eyes he would see before him *another* welsh rarebit and glass of milk and that he could eat and drink that *also*.

He opened his eyes, looked at the food and drink before him and proceeded to consume the lot — without the slightest difficulty.

John had been healed of the inability to swallow. The doubts that had been created in his mind and the belief that he would not be able to swallow, had been healed. In the relaxed state of hypnosis he accepted his healing and carried that healing forward into his normal, conscious state of mind. It was most important, when preparing John for the eating of the real food, to refer to the eating of the visualised food. In this way I created in his mind the 'fact' that, having done it once, there would be no problem in doing it again. When he had finished the real food and drink he was almost out of hypnosis. However, I went through the process of bringing him out of this happy, relaxed state and told him that there would now be no more problem with swallowing.

I made a tape recording for John. On it I helped him to go into hypnosis and visualise eating the food that was to be prepared for him by his mother. I suggested that he listened to this tape before every meal time and that there would be no problem with swallowing. In fact John did use the tape before each meal for a few days but then found that it was no longer necessary to use it on every occasion, so it was just used occasionally when he felt he needed a topping-up.

The laying on of hands continued and the tumour in John's head became smaller until there was almost nothing to show on the X-ray. John returned to a normal active life and began training for a career in the nursing profession.

Some months later, when all was going so well in John's life, it is sad to report that he had a massive brain haemorrhage and died.

From John's healing, knowledge was gained which has been used to great benefit in the healing of many others.

Breast Cancer

Alice, in her mid-fifties had had breast cancer which had been successfully dealt with by lumpectomy. She was having a check-up every four months. A recent examination had shown that there were two lumps in the left breast.

Within three weeks of seeing me she was due to see the surgeon who had performed the lumpectomy. The consultant explained that a return of the cancer could not be ruled out and he would write to the surgeon telling him of the latest condition.

She was in an acute state of stress and telephoned me for an appointment as soon as possible. The two lumps were certainly very much in evidence, so I gave the laying on of hands, first on her head, praying for the healing of her spirit, mind and body, then, that the power of God would wash her body clean of all malignancy. I next placed my hands on the breast. She told me that she felt a great heat coming from my hands and that the breast was throbbing. When the heat had subsided and the throbbing stopped I concluded the healing with a prayer of thanks.

The following day Alice telephoned me and told me that during the evening of the day of the healing, the breast began to throb again and become so hot that she was sure anyone standing in front of her would have been able to feel the heat! She went on to tell me that the breast had become dark, as though badly bruised. What had surprised her was the suddenness with which this had developed and that, within a couple of hours, it had resumed the normal state once again.

The following week she arrived for further healing when I noted that the lumps were still very much there. I did exactly the same when laying on hands, and it had exactly the same reaction when she was at home that evening.

The next appointment was the last opportunity to lay on hands before she saw the surgeon. However, this time I could find no lumps but we continued with the laying on of hands as before. She did not experience the usual heat and throbbing, neither did the breast react later in the day by becoming hot and discoloured.

I told her that I felt she could go for her appointment with the surgeon, confident that all was well. He examined her thoroughly and said that he could find no sign of a return of cancer. The lumps had gone.

When the surgeon asked Alice how she accounted for the sudden change in her condition, she told him that she had been receiving Christian healing during the previous three weeks.

"That explains it," said the surgeon, "I would like you to continue having healing. If you will do this I don't need to see you for a further six months."

We do not know what was in the letter he wrote to the consultant, but we did hear from his secretary that he had received a letter from the surgeon which contained "very good news" and that all was, indeed, well. This was later confirmed.

When I mentioned this case to a friend who is an oncologist, he said, "That is the sort of reaction we get sometimes when treating certain types of cancer with radiotherapy." He added, "It would appear that whatever power comes from your hands is similar to that used in radiotherapy." A nice thought, but I believe it to be far greater!

Colitis

The following brief account is typical of the many who have come to be relieved of serious bowel conditions:

In May 1982, I developed ulcerative colitis which gradually reduced my quality of life. The doctors said that there was no cure. The only treatment offered was tablets and it was, "See you in a month." Then it was two months and so it went on. Now and again I had a thorough examination.

In June of last year, I received the first laying on of hands and again in July when I attended my first Fellowship meeting. Because of the healing power of Jesus being channelled through the hands of the healer, I have never looked back. There is now nothing I will not attempt to do, whereas this time last year I was only a shadow of myself today. I thank God for Jesus and His gift of healing.

Dorothy wrote this account of her healing five years ago. Her life was governed by the location of toilets in her home town. The very thought of going out of her home and being unable to get to a toilet in time, was absolute torment. One can imagine her state of mind if she had ventured into a supermarket. She would have been trapped behind a queue of people at the check-out.

Such cases I approach in a similar manner to that which I approach food allergies. I am aware that the medical profession would smile at such a suggestion. But since people are made well by this approach — and surely they have the same objective for their patients — let us just thank God and continue to depend upon Him for His grace.

It may seem strange to some that different conditions can be healed by the same simple approach. When the mind is healed of its state of dis-ease and fear, there is no longer a reason for the condition. It is then that, through prayer and the laying on of hands, the physical effects of that condition are healed. I ask the sufferer to visualise, in hypnosis, eating a food which is wholly acceptable to them, one which they find enjoyable. A young man who was due to have a colostomy, enjoyed his porridge for breakfast so it was agreed that, as he visualised eating his porridge, I would lay hands on his throat and 'follow' the soothing, healing porridge through his body. As the porridge passed through his body, it 'healed' him. During the healing it was explained that the grain was "fed and watered by God's almighty hand". It was produced to nourish and to heal us... and that is exactly what it did for him and for so many others.

AIDS

When someone is terminally ill, and knows it, they are far more likely to be able to come to terms with the situation than those who are allowed to spend their last days in hope.

I remember the young man brought to Pin Mill from London by his devoted parents who were nursing him through the last weeks and days of his life. He had AIDS. After we had exchanged a few introductory remarks he said, 'It's not my body I'm worried about — it's my soul I'm concerned for.''

This young man knew he was about to die and wanted to ask for forgiveness of his sins. Before he arrived I wondered how I was going to approach his healing, but he made it so straightforward. I asked him if he would like me to lay hands on his head and anoint him with oil, asking Jesus Christ to forgive him all his sins — and that is exactly what I did.

I believe he left with a sense of peace. There was no follow-up, so I do not know what happened to him.

A Fertility Problem

The lady's name is Cherry and she was desperate to have a child. She first came to me a few days before she was due to have further surgery for the unblocking of her fallopian tubes. Previous surgery had proved unsuccessful and had left her in a highly nervous state in which to undergo more hospital treatment.

The story is best told by Cherry:

It was five years ago that I first met Jeff and Doreen at their beautiful, peaceful home in Pin Mill. I was feeling pretty low as I had already undergone gynaecological operations which had left me with adhesions blocking my fallopian tubes.

I was desperate to have a child and now all my hopes were based on yet another operation to free these adhesions. I was very frightened at the prospect of yet another anaesthetic and all the pain of a big operation.

At this, my first healing, I was immediately put at my ease and it was explained that in some cases, combining relaxation and visualisation with the laying on of hands can be of great benefit. I was shown how to relax and to visualise in this special way, which I found gave me a feeling of real peace in which to receive the laying on of hands.

Prayers were said for the success of the surgery, and that I need have no fear as "Jesus Christ was with me and all was well". I was then shown how to visualise going for the operation and taken through the most frightening stages, putting all my fears at bay. I was told that whenever I experienced fear I was to say, silently in my mind, "Jesus Christ is with me and all is well." I was also told that, with God's help, I definitely would have a child eventually. Hands were laid on my head and on my abdomen and I received a wonderful, peaceful healing. I felt so much better when I left Pin Mill and also very much more positive.

As it happened I certainly needed that healing because, after the operation, I haemorrhaged and nearly died. I was taken back into the operating theatre for more surgery the following morning and gradually made a good recovery. Unfortunately the tubes were still block-ed and after several more investigative operations my consultant told me there was nothing more he could do. Brian, my husband, and I were devastated. It seemed to me to be the end of the road. And yet somehow I was determined not to give in.

We went to Pin Mill again, and again I was given healing and told that "all would be well". This time I was helped to visualise the child that I would eventually have. The baby I saw was a girl. She was a little older than newborn, had a very little fair hair, blue eyes and was full of smiles. Jeff was so sure that I would conceive naturally and that I would be healed. This gave me such strength and a lift at a time when everyone else had given up on me.

IVF *(In Vitro Fertilisation)* is a method of helping infertile women to have children that I had only heard about through the media. I decided to do some research into it and, after discovering that there was an extremely long waiting list for this treatment on the NHS (about 2 to 3 years), I found a private clinic in London which only had a three month waiting-list. It was expensive but my father very kindly offered to pay for my treatment.

Throughout the treatment Brian and I were constantly in touch by 'phone with Jeff and Doreen who asked the Fellowship prayer chain to pray for us. Their endless patience, prayers and positive support meant so much to us. Whenever I felt a bit low or worried I would speak to my friends at Pin Mill on the 'phone and immediately feel so much better. Healing does work by 'phone!

In December 1985 the clinic confirmed that I was pregnant. Doreen was so eager to hear the news that she knew before Brian did as he was on tour with a play called *Doctor in House* and I couldn't phone him until the evening.

On my birthday, December 27, I had my first pregnancy scan and we saw two tiny little dots on the screen. These were my babies!

The pregnancy was difficult and I had a threatened miscarriage at eight weeks. But again I was reassured that all would be well, and on July 31, 1986, I gave birth to our darling twins, Christabel and Peter. I had to have a caesarean and was on life-support after the operation because I wasn't breathing. It was discovered later that I was allergic to the anaesthetic.

Christabel was 6lbs and Peter was 5lb 10oz. They were brought to me when I finally came round and were dressed in little white shawls and bonnets. They had to be kept in the special care baby unit for a few days because they were a month premature, but were brought regularly to me for feeding and were eventually allowed to stay with me.

Christabel had a shock of dark hair and very blue eyes and long eyelashes. Peter, who was so tiny was very fair and had no hair at all. I fed them myself for a year and they are now happy three-year-olds who have just started play school. Brian and I were so delighted when Jeff and Doreen agreed to be their Godparents because that is truly what they are.

So what happened, you may ask, to that little girl I had seen during that first relaxation, visualisation and healing?

Well, in October, 1988, the family were all ill with a sickness bug. I had it too but it did seem to go on rather longer than the others. To cut a long story short I discovered I was pregnant! My own hospital consultant was amazed. He, above all, knew after so many operations, what a mess my inside was in and thought that the nurses were playing a joke on him when he saw my name on the ante-natal list.

On June 30 this year (1991) I gave birth to our lovely little Rose. This time I had a caesarean with an epidural anaesthetic so that I could see her the moment she was born and would not have the problems I had before.

I spoke to Jeff the night before. As usual, he gave me such confidence and assured me that he and Doreen would be with me in thought, praying for me and that Jesus Christ was with us.

Rose weighed 8lbs 7oz. Although she had darkish hair when she was born, she now has very little hair which is very fair. She has beautiful blue eyes and smiles all the time — exactly like that baby I saw during that visualisation and prayer five years ago.

I know that healing works and that the prayers of my friends in the Pin Mill Fellowship have enabled the power of God to bring about a miracle not just for me but for many, many others. Brian and I thank them all from the bottom of our hearts.

Chapter 13

WORKING WITH
THE MEDICAL PROFESSION

When attending conferences on the healing ministry, there
has usually been a discussion on the subject of working with
the medical profession. The point that has been made is that
those in the medical profession do not take 'faith healing'
seriously and therefore avoid having anything to do with
what they, understandably, regard as fringe medicine and
merely anecdotal. In many cases this may be so, but it is
both encouraging and inspiring to be involved with doctors
who do truly recognise what can happen when God is given
a chance to heal.

A Doctor's Tribute

Dr Geoffrey Clark FRCP, Consultant Physician in
Rheumatology, expresses his thoughts on the way God may
be allowed to intervene to encourage the process of healing:

> As a rheumatologist I am often asked by patients about
> various complementary medicines. This is natural, as
> either they may be already using them or, since in a
> number of cases orthodox treatment cannot resolve their
> symptoms satisfactorily, they seek additional help. Many
> complementary systems have a long medical history, for
> example, herbalism and acupuncture. Whatever their
> origins, however, as orthodox doctors we do well to
> respect both those who are trained in them as well as our
> patients who feel inclined to seek help in this way. This
> is partly because our prime aim must be the patients'
> welfare and to decide, if their condition is improved,

189

how this has come about. We are also in a good position to provide an objective assessment of the effect on the illness and can often assist a patient in their decision as to whether to continue such treatment.

But health is not solely to do with the alleviation of measurable physical problems. The mind and the spirit of the person are also very much involved and if a person is feeling good in these areas they know it and it shows. As doctors, we have therefore, to think of our patients' lives in a wholistic way. This means that our concept of health is widened to include the person's relationships with themselves, with others, with God if they have a faith, and with the environment.

If one believes man has a soul, then clearly that soul is likely to be affected by any treatment whether spiritually based or not. However, if that soul is indeed implanted by God then the healing process could be influenced by Him. As a scientist, a doctor needs to keep an open mind as to the existence of God. The odds against the universe taking on the shape and composition that it has done with man as a product are many billions and billions to one against it happening. Had such a result occurred in an experiment, a scientist could certainly not dismiss it. As Clifford Longley concluded from such considerations, and Professor Stephen Hawking's study of the anthropic principle in "A Brief History of Time", the odds are on God's fine tuning of the universe. Other scientists have put it in a different way, regarding themselves as thinking God's thoughts after Him: a reverence for life was the key to Albert Schweitzer's development.

Therefore, if there is a system of healing which allows the possibility of God intervening to encourage the process, then I ought, as a doctor, to look at it as reasonably as I look at the complementary forms of medicine. It so happens that in the 20th century the Church has regained the concept of the early church, that healing was a distinct component of its work (Luke, Chapter 9: "Go preach and heal" is commanded three times by Jesus).

It has sacraments which promote healing, (e.g. Communion and the regular services as well as its important pastoral support and counselling at best), but it also has two other channels of healing, namely the laying on of hands and anointing. Both are designed to allow God to act in that situation, to encourage the natural healing processes, one could say, that He has already implanted. Therefore it has seemed natural as a doctor to refer those patients who seem to me most likely to respond to such an approach. There is little doubt that if such an approach is helpful in situations where doctors have come to the end of what we have to offer, then we ought to consider such referral much earlier and as part of the normal healing process. This might require careful discernment as to who should benefit — and counselling along with it.

It seemed fortunate to me that through various channels, I made the acquaintance of Esmond Jefferies. It so happened that this came at a time when a particular patient, the first I asked him to see, was suffering from a blood disorder. She had a very low platelet count as a consequence of her disease and the effects of drugs. She had excellent help from a haematologist yet her platelet count remained very low. Frequent transfusions were the order of the day. Therefore, especially as I had been caring for her for a long time and knew her well, I approached her and her husband to say that I believed it might be possible for God to change the course of her illness through someone I knew as a caring person and who gave the laying on of hands in a way which I felt was responsible, since he believed himself to be a channel of healing by God. I accompanied my patient and her husband on their visit to Mr Jefferies and witnessed his method of applying Christian healing ministry. Indeed, through the laying on of hands I was able to make my own contribution to it. There are many unanswered questions about the way in which this ministry works but this reflects more on the methods of investigation available to us rather than on the authenticity of it.

Primarily it is to do with healing and not necessarily cure physically. Nor is healing itself complete in an instant but part of a process of renewal towards wholeness and although space does not here permit descriptions, all those whom I have referred have experienced changes which have been helpful to their ongoing health. In the case of the patient with the low platelets, soon after her visit for healing and over a period of some years since, her platelet count has risen so that it no longer causes ill-effects.

As I have indicated, it is as relevant to remove bitterness and restore confidence in someone who otherwise would be able to cope physically. With residual physical problems, as often as not, people are given new insights, for example, they may find that they can, after all, embrace the orthodox treatment that has been suggested, and with renewed attitudes possibly respond all the better. Good communication is an important part of the preparation for healing and this includes all those who are concerned with the ongoing health of the person. I have always received a detailed, helpful, realistic report from Mr Jefferies in return. In this way one can be objective about progress and see more clearly the areas of improvement. When, as in the case of the patient with the low platelet count, an apparently unexplainable and, depending on one's definition of the word, miraculous change occurs, then this too can be appreciated the better. Appropriately carried out, the Christian healing ministry can work in partnership effectively with orthodox medicine. The scope for healing is widened thereby and the open, scientific mind should not find it too difficult to accept that the odds are in favour of God doing some fine tuning.

Working with Doctors

Recently, I had the privilege of being invited to talk to a meeting of the British Medical Association. The invitation came from the President of the particular division and I was billed as someone giving a talk on 'faith healing'

The first thing I did was to make quite clear that the term 'faith healing' was an umbrella title given to many different disciplines, and that I was concerned with that which Jesus Christ taught us to do.

It was interesting to observe the reactions. Some of the fifty doctors in the audience kept deadpan faces, while others began to develop smiles of encouragement and a few almost leaned forward in their chairs. For a moment I felt a bit like an evangelist, which was the last thing I wanted to do — so having made my point, I got straight on to the case studies which I felt would be of interest to them.

Whenever doctors are told stories of 'miraculous' healings their reply is almost always the same, "Merely anecdotal! Unless there is medical proof and I am given details of all medical treatment, I cannot accept such stories of healing."

On this occasion I made sure that no such comment could be made. I told of the healings of Ken and the cancer in his arm... of Russell and the healing of his blindness... and of Sharon and the healing of her fifteen years of deafness. The medical notes of all three were in their own local hospital and they could have access to all the information they required.

At this point I want to sound a note of caution. Christian healing should never be regarded as an *alternative* therapy. It is a means by which the grace of God is given to His children and which, in cases where orthodox treatment is being given, can complement that treatment for the good of the patient. God is in medicine just as He is in all other forms of healing in which caring, love and compassion are shown. He is in the work of the doctors and surgeons, the nurses and orderlies, and the ambulance drivers, just as He works through those who lay on hands in His name. I remember so well watching one of those fascinating television programmes, 'Your life in their hands'. It concerned a piece of major surgery. The camera went in close on the patient's body. The hand of the surgeon came into shot. It was holding a scalpel. The blade was about to make that first incision when the surgeon paused and the microphone picked up his voice, "I pray there is a greater hand than mine upon this scalpel." God and the surgeon were working as a team.

All too often people are referred for healing when the doctor can do no more. If only doctors would send their patients for healing as soon as orthodox treatment is commenced, patients would receive the benefit of all that can be done to help them.

When a patient receives the laying on of hands without first being referred by their doctor, it makes good sense for that patient to speak to their doctor and explain what has happened within Christian healing. If he is not kept in the picture he may, understandably, give credit for improvement in a condition to the medication. He may then change that medication to the disadvantage of the patient, making no allowance for the healing which has taken place through the laying on of hands, of which he would have been totally unaware. In such cases our role in Christian healing is to complement the treatment given by the medical profession. Where a good working relationship exists between the hospital, doctors and those involved in the healing ministry, it is helpful to all concerned that the doctors in charge of the case are aware that the patient is receiving the laying on of hands. In my experience, this is welcomed by most doctors who are then able to allow for the results of this ministry.

Recently, a lady who was diagnosed as having cancer in both breasts, was sent to me by her consultant to receive "as much healing as possible". He would then decide whether it was necessary to treat her by radiotherapy.

It has to be understood that doctors, and others within the medical profession, have arrived at their position in life through study based upon science. They gain confidence in a given treatment that can be repeated when given to other patients suffering from the same ailment and with the same results. If it cannot be repeated with any measure of certainty the doctor is unlikely to place any faith in it. On the other hand, when he runs out of orthodox treatments and can do no more for his patient, he is quite prepared to hand that patient over to receive the laying on of hands.

It is, therefore, understandable that most of the medical profession are highly suspicious of anyone without a scientific training. And unless they are committed Christians, they find it very difficult to accept that their patient can be 'cured' simply by prayer and the laying on of hands — and I do not blame them.

I respond to the medical profession in a manner which has been appreciated. When a consultant or GP refers a patient to me by letter or by telephone, I give a full written report on my meeting with his or her patient. In it I report on what I have learned about the background to the case, and give a detailed account of the healing and the manner in which the patient responded. When, as often happens, someone telephones me saying that doctor so-and-so told them to contact me, I see the patient, but unless there is a vitally important reason for doing so, I do not send a report to the doctor.

I have found that when visiting a terminal patient and

working alongside the doctor, it can be arranged that if the patient discusses the possibility of death with either of us, we communicate immediately. Then is the time to give prayers of reassurance, to talk freely of the splendour of the life to come, according to the promise made by Jesus. *Life begins at death* as Leslie Weatherhead says.

On one occasion I found that a wife had been told that her husband had inoperable cancer and the doctor had avoided telling him. The doctor told his wife that she could tell him if she wished to. Not surprisingly, she found it impossible to do this. When they came to me, this devoted couple were living a lie during the last days of their life together. It was left to me to handle the situation and when talking with the man I soon discovered that he suspected he had cancer and was reluctant to tell his wife. When the truth was known to both of them, all unnecessary tension left their relationship and the last days of their lives together were spent without deception to come between their love for each other. But doctors behaving in this way is, I am happy to say, a rarity.

Working with Hospitals

It sometimes happens that someone who has been receiving Christian healing together with orthodox treatment, is admitted to hospital, and they or their family have asked for the laying on of hands to be given to them on the hospital ward.

First it must be realised that, within the rules of the National Health Service, no one employed by the NHS — nurses and others who work with patients — is permitted to discuss a patient's faith with them. The only person who may talk of such matters is the hospital chaplain of whichever denomination the patient may be.

I cannot stress too strongly, the importance of going through the proper channels when dealing with hospitals — otherwise you will only meet opposition at every turn. This

I can promise you. But keep to the system, and you will find nothing but co-operation.

The senior chaplain has a responsibility to ensure that no 'fringe' or what may be considered 'undesirable' influences are brought to bear upon patients who will, in most cases, be emotionally vulnerable.

The first time I visited the hospital to give the ministry of healing to someone who had been coming to Pin Mill, I was confronted by the senior chaplain. He explained that he simply could not allow me to do so as this would open the door to many other who may well be involved in harmful, non-Christian practices. Whilst I understood his point, I nevertheless found it most frustrating and difficult to take.

Then came the day when the parents of a little girl with brain damage, asked the chaplain if he would agree to me giving her the laying on of hands. He agreed, subject to my having a talk with him before and explaining what I would be doing. At the end of our talk he asked if he may join me. We went to the ward where I met the parents and as they all stood around the bed, I placed my hands on the head of the child prayed aloud, in the name of Jesus Christ, for her healing. When the chaplain saw the manner in which I was giving the ministry, he gave me clearance to visit anywhere in the hospital. He asked that whenever I visited anyone, to let him know so that he could follow up on that patient. What better co-operation could one wish for?

Since that occasion I have been asked to give talks to The Catholic Guild of Nurses at the hospital and to the nurses on the main cancer ward — at Sister's request — so that they may understand what I am doing when I visit patients and draw the curtains around the bed. But as well as I now know that Sister, for she has been to Pin Mill a number of times, I always ask her permission before laying hands on anyone in her ward. In a number of cases I have been able to talk with the consultant about the patient before laying on hands. I cannot speak too highly of the help and co-operation I have received from the chaplain, doctors, nurses and staff of that hospital.

Epilogue

For all that has happened, is happening and yet to happen, let us give thanks to Almighty God for His Son, Jesus Christ, who has shown us the way to wholeness. Let us pray that we are led to believe His words, "I tell you the truth, anyone who has faith in me will do what I have been doing... And I will do whatever you ask in my name so that the Son may bring glory to the Father."

By offering healing prayer and laying on hands in His name, it is the wish of Jesus that the sick should be healed and that such healing, through the *Power* of the Holy Spirit, may bring *Glory* to His Father. When we truly believe, we may truly expect — and when we expect, great things can happen. For by following His example the blind can be given sight, the deaf be made to hear and the diseased be made clean. Praise the Lord! His is the power. Let His be the glory!